INTEGRATING THE CHARLESTON POLICE FORCE

INTEGRATING THE CHARLESTON POLICE FORCE

Stories of the Pioneers

EUGENE FRAZIER SR.

Published by The History Press
Charleston, SC
www.historypress.com

Copyright © 2020 by Eugene Frazier Sr.
All rights reserved

First published 2020

Manufactured in the United States

ISBN 9781467145206

Library of Congress Control Number: 2019956018

Notice: The information in this book is true and complete to the best of our knowledge. It is offered without guarantee on the part of the author or The History Press. The author and The History Press disclaim all liability in connection with the use of this book.

All rights reserved. No part of this book may be reproduced or transmitted in any form whatsoever without prior written permission from the publisher except in the case of brief quotations embodied in critical articles and reviews.

This book is a special tribute to all those pioneer African American men and women who served in law enforcement in Charleston County between the 1950s and the 1990s. Many were friends of mine. They suffered the frustration, humiliation and indignity of racism as they paved the way for generations to follow. Those who stuck with the job persevered and were able to retire. Those who were forced off the job—my hat goes off to them. It is truly sad to say that some of the young African American police officers of today do not have a clue as to what their predecessors endured for them to have the privileges they enjoy. Once again, I salute the men and women who have gone home to a Greater Glory to receive their final reward that only God can give. May those brothers and sisters rest in peace.

This book is also dedicated to Chief Silas Welch, Chief Mikey Whatley, Chief John H. Ball, Chief Walter Gay, Assistant Deputy Chief D.M. Boggs and my friend Ronald "Roddy" Perry, a former partner in the homicide division of the Charleston County Police Department and later chief of the Mount Pleasant Police Department. These men, despite living and working in the segregated South, were able to put aside their "white privilege" that they knew existed to see the potential in other men and to treat those men with respect despite their race. I raise my hat to them. May they all rest in peace.

CONTENTS

Introduction	9
1. City of Charleston Police Department	11
2. Charleston County Police/Sheriff's Office	23
3. Honors	87
Conclusion	107
Bibliography	109
About the Author	111

INTRODUCTION

Charleston, South Carolina, sits on the East Coast along the Atlantic Ocean between North Carolina and Georgia. Charleston is known by its citizens as the Holy City. It is a place deeply rooted in the Bible belt and prides itself on its tradition of southern hospitality. It is a city known for its brotherly and sisterly love shown to thousands of visitors and tourists as they walk along the streets. It is known for its cheerful greetings of "good morning" and "good evening" and smiles and nods that are typical of Charlestonians. However, before the 1970s, African Americans were not afforded this friendly treatment and hospitality; whites treated them as second-class citizens.

African Americans were voting in the 1960s, but there were spelling or history questions that were put in place that made it difficult for them to vote. Many African Americans were not able to pass these exams. The Voting Rights Act passed in 1965, following a prolonged protest of the court system at the local and state levels. The pressure came from the local National Association for the Advancement of Colored People (NAACP), its president J. Arthur Brown and other men, such as state senator Herbert U. Fielding, John Chisolm, John Cumming, Jack White, Reverend Cornelius Campbell of St. James Presbyterian Church on James Island and many others. Numerous meetings were held over the years with the late mayors William Morrison and Palmer Gaillard Jr. and other influential white leaders, concerning the plight of African Americans. In 1950, the City of Charleston, under Chief William F. Kelly, and because

Introduction

Senator Herbert U. Fielding. *Courtesy of Frederick Fielding.*

of pressure from the NAACP and the courts, hired the first group of African American police officers. However, second-class status remained the norm for these police officers and all African American citizens.

During the 1950s and 1960s, African American city police officers were not allowed to arrest white citizens. If a black officer apprehended a white citizen who was violating the law, he could only detain that person until a white officer took over. Black policemen were also not allowed to drive patrol cars. They were dropped off for their walking beats in the city limits by a white officer in a patrol car.

Many of these offensive policies began to change during the 1969 Medical College Hospital strike, when nurses and hospital workers walked off their jobs. The strike was no surprise to African Americans who were familiar with Charleston's history of oppression. This was the city where the Civil War began when the first shot was fired on Fort Sumter, and South Carolina was the first state to secede from the Union. The primary goal of white Charlestonians during the nineteenth century was to preserve the institution of slavery. A majority of white citizens were proud of this distinction, though many claimed that slavery was not the reason for the war. However, historians have proven them wrong.

Other improvements in the policies of the police departments of the city and county of Charleston took even longer to accomplish and demanded great fortitude by a number of individuals, both black and white. I've been proud to be a part of some of those struggles and described them in my 2001 book *From Segregation to Integration: The Making of a Black Policeman*. But I want to give particular credit to many of the individuals who were part of the struggle to bring positive change to the area police departments. In the following pages, that is exactly what I will do.

Note: All of the victims' names and addresses have been changed to protect them and their families, including the fictitious name of "Tom Anderson," which was changed to protect his family.

1
CITY OF CHARLESTON POLICE DEPARTMENT

In 1950, Chief William F. Kelly hired the City of Charleston Police Department's first group of African American police officers. There were eight men in that esteemed group: Officers Bennie Taylor, Cambridge Jenkins, George H. Gathers, Monkue Henegan, Ernest Deveaux, Christopher B. Ward, Walter Burke and James L. Mikell.

I knew James L. Mikell for most of his career and worked closely with him. Mikell was about forty-four years old when I met him. He was about five-foot-seven, with a slender built and a medium brown complexion. He was in good physical shape. He graduated from Shaw University in North Carolina and was married to Jewel Mikell, who taught high school. They had one son. Mikell was soft spoken and had a professional demeanor—a no-nonsense individual. He was considered a father to many of the officers. He would listen and give his opinion and advice. During a number of interviews and conversations, he helped me understand the experiences of the city's first black officers.

"Frazier," he said to me, "when the first groups of us were hired in 1950, besides our police training, some of the first instructions we received from supervisors was that, as black policemen, we were not allowed to arrest white people.

"We were told, 'If for any reason you have to arrest a white person violating a city ordinance or state law, y'all need to hold them and call for a

Integrating the Charleston Police Force

Chief William Kelly. *Courtesy of U.S. deputy marshal Fred Stroble.*

white officer in a squad car, by pulling the telephone alarm box, to pick up the prisoner. You guys are not allowed to drive squad cars, only ride in one to and from police headquarters to your walking beat and back.' We were not allowed to walk beats in predominately white communities—for example, south of Calhoun Street, Broad Street and South Battery. These were the areas where the blue bloods, the rich, the well-to-do white people lived."

Mikell continued, "Frazier, one day I was walking the beat between Line and King Streets. There was a bar on the corner operated by a Jewish gentleman. I don't recall his name. Around 1:00 a.m., a white man came out of the bar apparently very intoxicated, standing in the middle of the street. I ordered him out of the street before he was run over by a car. When I approached him, he said, 'No nigger police going to tell me what to do.'

"At that moment, he swung at me with a right fist. I blocked the blow and took my nightstick and chopped him a few times until I got him under control and handcuffed him. Upon arrival of the squad car, the sergeant wanted to know why I arrested a white man and why he was bleeding. I told him I did not give a damn what color a man was, if the SOB tried to hurt me, that's exactly what he will get. He booked me on report several times over the years and told me, although I had a college degree, he would never recommend me for a detective position."

"The 1950s were a tough time for us during the winter months when it was cold," Mikell said. "The people that knew us on our beats would let us come inside their homes and get warm. Some even left their screen doors unlocked for us during the cold and rainy nights. Sometimes, when the squad supervisor drove by a corner where I should be, he would raise hell asking where I was. One morning at the end of my shift, I had enough. I told him if we were allowed to drive squad cars like the white officers, he would not have to ask me that question. I was fed up with the crap and did not give a damn whether I was terminated. The sergeant's response was, 'That could be arranged.'"

Group of African American Police Officers, 1963. *Front row, left to right*: Detective Josey Wong and Detective Christopher Ward. *Second row*: Detective Melvin Simmons, Officer Paul Green, unidentified officer, unidentified officer and Officer Harry B. Smith. *Third row*: Officer McWilliams and Sergeant Walter Burke. *Fourth row*: Officer Scott, Detective Fred Strobel, unidentified officer, Officer Wilber Burgess and Detective Monkue Henegan. *Courtesy of Deputy Chief Jerome Taylor.*

Integrating the Charleston Police Force

Detective James L. Mikell.
Courtesy of Mikell family.

Mikell was surprised when Chief Kelly called him and George Gathers into his office and promoted both of them to detectives. Mikell said, "Between 1955 and 1962, the black detectives on duty were allowed to drive the one car that was reserved for us on each shift. Following our promotions, Detective Gathers and I solved many high-profile cases in Charleston and continued to receive recognitions, but when the promotion list came down, only the white officers were promoted.

"We continued to live with racial insults from white supervisors. In 1962, I had enough of the disrespect and decided to resign from the Charleston City Police Department. I joined the Charleston County Police Department, and George Gathers would soon join me, where we were hired as detectives by Chief Silas Welch."

In 1955, Josey Wong and Cambridge Jenkins were the first two uniformed policemen promoted to detectives in the city police department. In 1962, they were both hired by J. Pete Strom, chief of the South Carolina Law

Enforcement Division (SLED), on the recommendation of then-governor Ernest "Fritz" Hollings. This made them the first two African Americans to serve as SLED agents in South Carolina. However, not long after Donald S. Russell was elected governor in 1966, he fired both in what was clearly a political move. Both Wong and Jenkins returned to Charleston. Wong was rehired by the Charleston City Police Department as a detective, and Jenkins would later be hired by the U.S. Marshal Service, making him the first black deputy U.S. marshal from South Carolina.

Melvin Simmons, Walter Burke, James L. Mikell and Fred Strobel were the four intellectual gentlemen who I witnessed in my early years of law enforcement. They stood out among their peers. Burke was the first African American to be promoted to the supervisor's rank of sergeant in the city police department's uniform division. However, during the 1950s and through the late 1960s, he was only allowed to supervise black police officers.

If someone were to ask me who I thought stood out as the best African American police officer during those turbulent years of policing, it would be a difficult question to answer. The names of Sergeant Walter Burke, Detective James L. Mikell, Detective Melvin Simmons, Detective Cambridge Jenkins, Detective Fred Strobel and Detective George Gathers would be at the top of the list. But, in the end, I would have to select James L. Mikell because of his approach, demeanor and politeness when addressing African Americans during those difficult years.

I KNEW FRED STROBEL for most of his law enforcement career and worked with him in the federal district courts for eight years, but I first met him in 1962, before I started my career in law enforcement. He was the second black motorcycle police officer for the City of Charleston Police Department. The first officer was Tracey Oliver. I met Fred after I was discharged from the army. One day, I saw Fred sitting on his motorcycle between Esau Jenkins Restaurant and the James Hotel. During that time, these were the only places, besides the Brooks Motel and Restaurant on Morris Street, that black entertainers could frequent.

I approached Fred and told him of my desire to become a police officer. He realized that I might have an issue with the city police department because of its discriminatory policy that did not allow black officers to arrest white citizens. He also understood that due to my service in the army as a drill sergeant and my leadership over white recruits, this would indeed present a problem. Therefore, he suggested that I may want to consider joining the Charleston County Police Department instead of the city police department because the county did not have this discriminatory policy. As a result of this conversation, I later joined the Charleston County Police Department.

Fred was about five-foot-ten with a medium complexion and a slender built. He was quiet and reflective—more of an introvert in nature and a no-nonsense person. If asked a question, Fred would think about it before responding. His attendance at LaSalle University certainly contributed to his reflective and thoughtful responses. During interviews and conversations with him, he said to me, "Gene, I was hired in 1962 by the city police department during Mayor Palmer Gaillard's administration. William F. Kelly was chief of police. As you already know, during those early years, black policemen were not allowed to drive squad cars. We had to walk in the rain and cold weather. I was one of the first two black officers appointed to the Motorcycle Squad. From there, I was promoted to the rank of detective where I handled a number of high-profile cases, but, because of continued racial discrimination against African Americans, I resigned about 1968."

By the time Fred resigned, Chief Kelly had left the City of Charleston Police Department and had been elected sheriff of Charleston County. After his resignation in 1968, Fred reached out to Sheriff Kelly, who hired him, this time as the first black deputy sheriff in Charleston County.

"I continued to work there until 1972," Fred said. "In 1972, I took the U.S. Civil Service examination and scored ninety-six out of a possible score of one hundred and was appointed deputy U.S. marshal. I would be the third from South Carolina and the second black deputy U.S. marshal from Charleston. I paired up with Deputy Marshal Cambridge Jenkins.

"From the beginning, the racial discrimination and the hostile environment in the Marshal Service, as well as in the public arena, were just as bad as the police department. Jenkins and I continued to excel in our job performances and other areas. However, when the time came for promotions, we were left out. Jenkins and I had more education than many of our white counterparts, but that did not matter." Fred, as mentioned earlier, attended Lasalle University, completing some courses but did not graduate. Jenkins graduated from Palmer College.

"Gene," Fred continued, "I recall Jenkins and I were dispatched on an assignment in Nashville, Tennessee, to escort three white male prisoners for delivery to the federal district court in Charleston. Upon identifying ourselves as deputy United States marshals, a white female in the office said to us, she never thought the day would come when two black men were

Detective Fred Strobel with Detective Christopher Ward and Ward's wife. *Courtesy U.S. deputy marshal Fred Stroble.*

allowed to arrest white men. She said it in a manner that let us know she did not like it.

"As other blacks entered the U.S. Marshal Service, they experienced hostile environments and racial tension. Gene, it got so bad all over the United States that blacks in the U.S. Marshal Service organized a Black Marshal Organization and filed a lawsuit against the Marshal Service. Wallace Roney from Washington, D.C., was elected chairman of the organization. They sued the Justice Department for encouraging discrimination against blacks in the Marshal Service.

"A white ex-chief deputy marshal's wife testified in U.S. district court in Washington, D.C., on behalf of the black marshals about the plot to deny blacks promotions. U.S. district judge Gerhard Gesell heard the case and awarded the black marshals actual and punitive damages of $4 million. Many of the African Americans that joined the U.S. Marshal Service during that period of racial discrimination resigned and sought employment elsewhere.

"Gene, although the first three black marshals from South Carolina were denied promotions," Fred continued, "all three of us retired with over twenty years of service. I spent ten years in state courts and forty years with the federal court system. I finally got my promotion with the help of U.S.

Integrating the Charleston Police Force

U.S. Deputy marshal Fred Stroble with Senator Ernest "Fritz" Hollings. *Courtesy of U.S. deputy marshal Fred Stroble.*

marshal Lidia Glover, and I retired as a GS-13 deputy marshal. Following my retirement from the Marshal Service, I began another career as a court security officer for the federal district court in Charleston, located at the corner of Broad and Meeting Streets, where you and I worked together until I retired."

Fred Strobel and Wilbur Burgess are the last two African American men who were hired as police officers in the city of Charleston during the 1950s and early 1960s who were still alive during the writing of this book. Unfortunately, Fred went on to be with the Lord on February 2, 2019. I was one of the speakers at his wake on February 7. I attended Fred's funeral on February 8, 2019. All of the speakers captured the essence of who Fred was as a man and as a friend. But Fred was a quiet man, and to capture the other part of him—the part of family man and father—I have included the words spoken by his youngest daughter, Yolanda Stroble Mason, at his funeral. Her words are as follows:

> *There are so many things I can say about my dad. I can tell you my dad was the epitome of God's unconditional love for man. My dad lived a life of repentance and rest. He helped people who had done wrong, but their error stayed right there. You could rest assure that he would not say a word after helping someone. His acts of kindness demonstrated and exemplified the love God has for us through the Lord Jesus Christ. As I saw my dad give to and help people countless times, I can say he lived the scripture I Peter 4:8 "Love covers a multitude of sins."*
>
> *My dad was an encourager and always saw the best in people. He encouraged always! My dad was a no-nonsense peaceful man.*
>
> *My dad kept the faith! Many times, he shared with me and so many how the grace of God kept him on many dangerous assignments. He would always encourage me with Hebrews 11:1, "Now faith is the substance of things hoped for, the evidence of things not seen." He would then send me handwritten notes that read "Keep the Faith." I wholeheartedly believe the events of this last week have strengthened my faith. As I was there when*

my dad took his last breath, my faith in God and His love and peace, even through challenging times, has been made real to me. II Corinthians 5:8, "To be absent from the body is to be present with the Lord," has given me comfort and strength.

In the days ahead, I admonish you to love unconditionally, repent and rest, encourage daily and keep the Faith!

I left that funeral with peace in my heart, knowing that my friend has now gone home to be with the Lord. He understood who his God is and who kept him all these years. Fred served Him on Earth, and he will worship Him in Heaven.

RUBIN MACK SR. WAS among the second group of African American men hired as police officers by the Charleston City Police Department. Rubin was hired in 1959 and retired in 1980. He began a second career with the U.S. Marshal Service as a chief security officer (CSO) at Broad and Meeting Streets. I knew Rubin for most of his police career. I had the privilege of working with him on investigations that revealed suspects who were committing crimes that connected the jurisdictions of the city and county police departments.

I recall that Detective George Gathers and I assisted Rubin and other city detectives in reference to the robbery and murder of Josef Molf in 1972 at his liquor store on President Street. Detective Gathers and I, along with a team of city detectives, went to the residence of one of the suspects, Reginald Mack. George, Rubin and I went into Mack's bedroom early that morning to arrest him. Detective David Zorn and the other city officers surrounded the house. In Reginald Mack's bedroom, Detective Gathers placed his .38-caliber revolver to Mack's head. Meanwhile, Rubin woke Reginald Mack from his sleep while reaching under his pillow, where he found and removed a revolver.

Following the last day of the trial in the court of general sessions, Detective Gathers and I escorted Reginald Mack to the county jail while the city detectives escorted the second defendant, James Alston. I recall asking Mack why he shot Josef, a good man who had helped many black people who lived in an area referred to as "Back da Green" in the Gadsden Green Project.

Reginald Mack looked at us and replied, "I'd probably do the same thing to you."

Integrating the Charleston Police Force

Left: Detective Rubin Mack. *Courtesy of Steven Mack.*

Right: Detective Sergeant George Gathers. *Courtesy of Gathers family.*

Detective Gathers said, "Reggie, you better watch your mouth. You just threatened two police officers. You really don't want to do that. You might want to live a little longer."

Detective Rubin Mack was one of the detectives assigned to investigate Attorney George Payton's 1975 murder during the early days of the case. I describe the case in much more detail in my book *From Segregation to Integration: The Making of a Black Policeman*. I explained that I had been following Payton's career since 1966, and I found him to be "an ambitious proud black man who was looking to achieve greatness....I believe that Payton had that special vision and courage that many black leaders before his time possessed." And he wasn't afraid. In 1968, he ran for U.S. Congress against the long-term and very powerful congressman L. Mendel Rivers.

After investigating Payton's murder, Detective Gathers and I suggested to the city detectives that Payton had been killed by a professional hit man. Later, the two city detectives told Captain Walter Edwards about our belief. Edwards then told our supervisor, Captain Richard F. Grassie, that he did not want George and me to work on the case.

My conclusion about Payton being killed by a professional was partly due to his work on a land transaction on Hilton Head Island, about which he had received threatening phone calls. I happened to be in his office on a

City of Charleston Police Department

City police officers, 1972. *First row, left to right*: Detective Ray Shoke, Detective Grady Craven, Lieutenant Tillman, Captain Walter Edward, unidentified male, Detective Captain Tracy Oliver, Ms. Thelma Ellington, unidentified female and Ms. McWilliams. *Second row*: unidentified male, unidentified male, Detective Ruben Mack, Detective Desmond Duc, Detective Scruggin, unidentified male and female. *Third row*: Detective Sergeant Paul Davis, Detective Sergeant Conklin, Detective Robert Scott and Detective Josey Wong. *Fourth row*: Detective Robert Horsley, Detective Buist, Detective Charles Salsbury, Detective Charlie Temple and Detective Christopher Ward. *Courtesy of Rubin Mack.*

different case when I heard him respond to one of those threats. Through further investigation with Payton's secretary, I found that the gun must have had a silencer because she only heard a thud—no gunshot. A silencer would be characteristic of the type of weapon used by a professional hitman. Despite our concerns, Detective Gathers and I were abruptly taken off the case and were told that county detectives were forbidden from any further involvement in the Payton murder investigation. The case remains unsolved to this day. I'm convinced that a professional hitman murdered Attorney Payton. I think that's also the key reason why Payton's murder remains unsolved.

Integrating the Charleston Police Force

PFC Woodrow Singelton. *Courtesy of Aletha Singelton.*

WOODROW SINGELTON WAS THE first African American from James Island hired by the City of Charleston Police Department. He graduated from W. Gresham Megget High School, which was the very first African American high school built on James Island, in 1953. He was assigned to the Traffic Division Motorcycle Squad, where he was promoted to private first class and worked in the traffic division until he was medically retired in 1985, after twenty years of honorable service.

2
CHARLESTON COUNTY POLICE/ SHERIFF'S OFFICE

Charleston County chief Silas B. Welch hired the first group of African American policemen during those trying and difficult years of segregation in the 1960s. Chief Welch was not popular with some of the politicians in the county because he went against the wishes of many whites who did not want African Americans in law enforcement. He was a good and decent man. Welch hired me as the first African American police officer from James Island. He was hired by Chief J. "Pete" Strom of the State Law Enforcement Division after his retirement from the force.

After my discharge from the United States Army in 1961, I returned to Charleston. I had served six years in the army, including a sixteen-month tour in Korea. I rose to the rank of sergeant E-6 and received an honorable discharge. I submitted applications to the Charleston County Police Department, South Carolina State Troopers, South Carolina State Law Enforcement Division (SLED), United States Postal Service and the Charleston Naval Shipyard. I received an offer from the City of Charleston Police Department, but I refused. I was aware of the policy that black officers were not allowed to arrest white people. I was not going to work in a place where I could not arrest a person accused of committing a crime simply based on the color of his or her skin.

The first response from my employment applications came from the South Carolina Highway Patrol. It stated that the background investigation, which included my military experience and education, qualified me for the job. However, it regretted to inform me that since I was only five feet, seven

INTEGRATING THE CHARLESTON POLICE FORCE

Patrolman Eugene Frazier Sr. *Courtesy of author.*

inches tall, I failed to meet its minimum height requirement of five feet, eight inches for police officers. But I knew this was not true because I knew a white state trooper who was only five feet tall who patrolled the Charleston, Colleton and Beaufort County areas. The South Carolina Highway Patrol still refused to hire African Americans.

In 1965, I received notifications from the U.S. Post Office, Charleston Naval Shipyard and the Charleston County Police Department, all informing me that I qualified for these positions. I chose the Charleston County Police Department. I was among the first group of African American men hired by the county police department and the first from James Island. I had no

Charleston County Police / Sheriff's Office

problem with my police training due to my military background. Charleston County's jurisdiction began at the Georgetown County line north of McClellanville and stretched to the Colleton County line on U.S. Highway 17 South. It was approximately ninety-five miles long and had a width that stretched some twenty-five miles to Berkeley County.

There were only fifty-six men on the force when I joined. The department had no written policy preventing black police officers from arresting white people. We could arrest anyone violating the county and state laws. The county's policy for patrolling allotted only one police officer for an evening or midnight shift in Mount Pleasant to the Georgetown County line—some forty-five miles from Charleston. This policy was the same for the area from West Ashley to the Colleton County line. If a black police officer was working in any of the county districts from the West Ashley to the Colleton County areas or Georgetown to Mount Pleasant areas and no white officer was available, he had to answer the call. However, there were some older white supervisors who tried to discourage us by using discriminatory tactics. There was a lack of respect for African Americans in the department, and racism ran rampant. However, there were some white men during those early years who believed in common decency. I can recall three of them in those early years. They were Sergeant Johnny Smart, Sergeant Emery Bee and Detective Michael Whatley. I have never heard any of them use racial slurs or seen them be disrespectful toward African Americans in my presence.

State Trooper and U.S. marshal Israel Brooks. *Courtesy of Nadine Brooks.*

IN 1967, I RECEIVED a call from Israel Brooks Jr., a friend of mine. I had met Israel several years earlier. He was a veteran of the U.S. Marine Corps and was from Newberry, South Carolina. He informed me that he had been hired by the South Carolina Highway Patrol and was working in the Beaufort and Colleton County area. He suggested that we could meet while we were both working near the Colleton/Charleston County line. We would often eat together at Alex's Restaurant in West Ashley. Israel would become the first African American state trooper. He worked his way through the promotional process to the rank of major before his retirement. In 1994, Israel Brooks was the first African American appointed to U.S. marshal from South Carolina. President William J. Clinton appointed him based on the recommendation of U.S. senator Ernest "Fritz" Hollings.

TILLMAN MILLHOUSE WAS AMONG the first three African American men hired as state troopers in South Carolina in 1971. As noted in a proclamation for the town of Summerville on February 7, 2019, Tillman remains the oldest living person of color with the most seniority and the only African American appointed as a special deputy U.S. marshal among fifty-one South Carolina Highway Patrol troopers. Tillman was married to Emily Myers Millhouse for fifty-three years, and they were blessed with four children and seven grandchildren. They were happily married until her passing in 2011. Tillman and I met again to celebrate the life of our friend Fred Stroble. We spoke about the amazing life of Fred, a man dedicated to making a difference in the field of law enforcement.

PFC Tillman Millhouse. *Courtesy of Tillman Millhouse.*

SOMETIMES, VARIOUS OFFICERS WOULD get together for lunch or dinner at different locations. Many of these meetings would take place at a Krispy Kreme—either the Rivers Avenue or West Ashley locations. We also met at Alex's Restaurant on Dorchester Road, in West Ashley and in Mount Pleasant. One particular meeting occurred on a Friday night in June 1967, when I was working the 11:00 p.m. to 7:00 a.m. shift. I was working the East Cooper district, and it was around 3:00 a.m. when Patrolman Hoke Jones and I met at the Alex's Restaurant on Coleman Boulevard to eat an early morning breakfast.

Alex's was the only place open during those hours, with the exception of Piggy Park Restaurant in Mount Pleasant. A white male who appeared intoxicated was creating a disturbance as we sat down to eat. He walked over to our table and asked what a "nigger policeman" was doing with a white

PFC Tillman Millhouse with Deputy Chief Jerome Taylor. *Courtesy of Tillman Millhouse.*

man. Needless to say, he was arrested by that same "nigger policeman." The manager of the restaurant told me that she was glad we arrested him. She said that he was a Klansman and a troublemaker.

Integrating the Charleston Police Force

My years as a police officer left many lasting impressions, but one day was etched in my mind forever—September 21, 1967, just two years after I started with the Charleston County Police.

I was working the 7:00 a.m. to 3:00 p.m. shift. Detectives James L. Mikell, George Gathers and I were in the outer detective's office of the Charleston County Police Department. The supervisor and second-in-command of the detectives Sergeant William Skinner, a white officer who stood six feet, three inches tall and weighed 240 pounds, came in the outer detective's office at about 9:00 a.m. and ordered Detective Gathers into his office. The door closed behind them. Mikell and I could not hear everything that was being said, but we did hear Sergeant Skinner yelling at Detective Gathers about being late for work. Detective Gathers told Skinner he was not a child and was not going to be treated like one and attempted to leave the office. But Sergeant Skinner grabbed Detective Gather's coat, causing it to rip.

Sergeant Skinner continued to hold George's coat and called him "boy," telling him not to walk away.

Detective Gathers spun around and told Skinner to turn him loose Sergeant Skinner refused. Detective Gathers then punched Skinner with a left and followed with a right jab to the head, sending Skinner reeling to the floor. Detective Mikell grabbed Detective Gathers and pushed him out the door.

I grabbed Sergeant Skinner, who was on his knees and appeared disoriented. He reached for his revolver. He yelled for me to turn him loose and shouted to Lieutenant Rudolph Knight, who was in charge of the detective division, that he wanted that "nigger" locked up for assaulting him.

Gathers was suspended from the department. Sergeant Skinner did not know that Detective Gathers was a boxer, and no one had ever defeated him in the local boxing arena. Nicknamed "Puggy George," Detective Gathers was roughly the same size as Sergeant Skinner. Later that day, Detective Mikell said to me, "Frazier, remember what you just witnessed here today. You are going to see many more of these abuses and racism during your career. It will be up to those of you who survive to change the racial culture in this department."

I will never forget the racial abuses that black people suffered in the following decades. I would suffer those abuses and other forms of racism as well.

ONE HORRIFIC SITUATION INVOLVED being targeted and set up by command staff officers in the department. They charged me with wrongdoing in the investigation of a murder case, but the grand jury's decision was that it was a departmental matter, and I was not indicted. Those command officers knew this from the beginning because Magistrate Margie Cannon had already signed a warrant for the informant's arrest but was holding it in abeyance, pending the informant's cooperation during the homicide investigation. This was a common practice used by detectives during those years. Informants who committed crimes and were willing to give information on other crimes, such as murders, robberies and rapes, would sometimes cooperate with the police for a lighter sentence through the solicitor's office and their attorneys. That procedure is still being used by police. I knew why these trumped-up charges and other allegations were being alleged against me, but I will elaborate on that later.

Two months after this, Charleston County council chairman J. Mitchell Graham ordered the police chief to reinstate Detective George Gathers. Gather's reinstatement was due to political pressure and county council members' review of the facts surrounding the incident.

During a 1969 trial in Charleston County Court, Sergeant Skinner would make his famous racial remark belittling the Filipino race. He called the Filipino people low class and stated that they lived like animals. The trial judge chastised him for his racial views. That same year, Chief Silas B. Welch promoted Corporal Walter Gay to the position of lieutenant over Sergeant Skinner. Skinner resigned from the department and sought employment elsewhere. But prior to leaving, Sergeant Skinner would be involved in a robbery case where he could have cost an innocent man his freedom. That case is outlined later. Shortly after that, Chief Welch accepted a position with SLED and resigned from the force in 1970. His retirement was effective in 1971. When the first opening became available for an agent position, Welch wanted to know if I was interested in the job. Since I had eleven years seniority with the county, I recommended Walter Mitchell for the position.

IT WAS JULY 1967. I was a uniform patrolman. That day, I was assisting Detectives Gathers and Mikell when the three of us were summoned to Chief Welch's office. He informed us that he had a request for a security detail to protect Dr. Martin Luther King Jr. This request came from Charleston County Council but was prompted by J. Arthur Brown, local president of the NAACP, and Esau Jenkins. Both J. Arthur Brown and Esau Jenkins were

Integrating the Charleston Police Force

known for their work as civil rights activists. However, J. Arthur Brown was more well known because his work was visible and often documented in television, newspapers and other public arenas.

J. Arthur Brown would become known for filing the lawsuit for his teenage daughter Minerva to attend Rivers High School. Rivers was an all-white high school in downtown Charleston. Unfortunately, Minerva graduated from high school before the lawsuit was heard. It was her sister, Millicent, who ended up attending Rivers High School. The case is known as *Millicent Brown et al v. Charleston County School Board, District 20*. Millicent and Minerva went on to lives dedicated to improving the lives of African Americans, particularly in the field of education. The Brown legacy continues.

Esau Jenkins was often in the shadows and was better known by African Americas in rural areas, particularly Johns Island. He was often referred to as Charleston's Dr. Martin Luther King. There were no buses to transport African American children to schools in Charleston during this time, so Mr. Jenkins got a Volkswagen bus and did it himself.

Left to right: Millicent Brown, Geraldine F. Minter and Minerva Brown. *Courtesy of Geraldine F. Minter.*

The world can now learn of this great man in the corridors of the National Museum of African American History and Culture in Washington, D.C. The back hatch of his Volkswagen bus, featuring the words "Love is Progress, Hate is Expensive," that transported so many African American children to public schools now sits in the museum as a testament to the strength and resilience of these men and so many others.

Brown and Jenkins kept fighting for equality and justice throughout their lives. They both left behind a legacy of civil rights work dedicated to improving the lives of African Americans in Charleston. They were proactive in the fight for justice for the African Americans in this city. They did not wait to make changes. They became the changemakers in a city that still does not understand the determination, strength and love that these men possessed to make those changes. Unfortunately, very few Charlestonians—especially the young—know about these heroes of the Charleston civil rights movement. It is one of the tragedies of the South—the tragedy of not knowing and honoring their African American heroes. It is a tragedy that can and must be corrected.

J. Arthur Brown. *Courtesy of Lowcountry Digital Library, Avery Research Center at the College of Charleston.*

On that day in July 1967, Chief Welch said Dr. King should be arriving at the Charleston Municipal Airport on July 29. He wanted Gathers, Mikell and me, in addition to SLED, to pick Dr. King up from the airport and escort him to Charleston County Hall on King Street for a speaking engagement. We were to remain with him for the duration of his visit. Also, we were to ensure his safety until he boarded his plane. Chief Welch added that since I was a veteran of the Korean War, I was to check out a rifle with a scope in addition to my sidearm. He added that if any harm came to Dr. King while in his county, he would hold the three of us personally responsible, and we would be fired. We assured the chief that no harm would come to Dr. King while he was in our care. Subsequently, Dr. King flew out of Charleston safely.

Integrating the Charleston Police Force

ANOTHER RACIAL INCIDENT THAT I will never forget occurred on April 4, 1968. I was on special assignment patrolling the Wadmalaw/Johns Island area from 6:00 p.m. to 2:00 a.m. Patrolman Jesse Williams was assigned the North Charleston area, and Patrolman James Owens was assigned the Edisto, Ravenel and Hollywood areas. I vividly recall it was sometime between 7:30 p.m. and 8:30 p.m. when I was traveling across the bridge that separates John's Island from Wadmalaw Island. Sergeant Charlie Grooms's, the supervisor of uniform patrol division, voice came over the police radio, calling Lieutenant Cannady and advising him that they finally got that rabble rouser. Lieutenant Cannady asked Sergeant Grooms who he was talking about. Grooms said Dr. King, that civil rights troublemaker. He had just been killed in Memphis, Tennessee. Jesse came over the radio and asked Patrolmen Owens and me to meet him at Main Road and Highway 17 in Red Top.

The three of us were upset. Jesse was a religious man, but that night, he could not hold back his anger. He said to us, "Did you hear what that SOB said about Dr. King, calling him a rabble rouser and a troublemaker and being glad that he was killed?" I told Jesse I too was angry, but we had to wait for our time to act.

Chief Paul F. Hartline

Paul F. Hartline was appointed chief of the Charleston County Police Department in 1970, after the retirement of Chief Silas B. Welch. My first meeting with Hartline impressed me. He was a man of very few words who got right to the point. He was impeccable with his dress. His military style, including his crew cut and demeanor, reminded me of Sergeant Vince Carter, played by Frank Sutton in the television series *Gomer Pyle, U.S.M.C.*

During Hartline's tenure, I asked permission from the squad sergeant to see Lieutenant Rudolph Knight to request permission to assist the detectives in following up investigations. Lieutenant Knight gave me permission as long as the squad sergeant approved it.

One of the cases to which I was assigned involved a robbery in April 1970. A uniformed patrol officer contacted headquarters and stated that a lone black male armed with a sawed-off rifle entered the office of the Americana Motel on Spruill Avenue and demanded money—allegedly about $500—from the clerk. He also took the clerk's purse, which contained her personal documents and numerous other items. E.A. Beck, a white detective, was assigned to the case. The description of the Americana Motel suspect matched the description of a suspect who Detectives George Gathers, Jesse Williams and I had identified in several armed robbery cases in the Charleston County area. We were helped by an informant, but we did not have enough probable cause to make an arrest. Detective Gathers and I received information that Detective Beck was about to arrest a black male from the Union Heights area, using a biased photographic lineup.

Gathers and I were concerned because we had witnessed Beck talking in a condescending manner to black personnel, and in conversations he often referred to blacks as inferior. Gathers and I also heard him refer to blacks as "niggers." He did not seem to care if we heard. The political climate at that time gave him this confidence.

Beck's supervisor at the time was Sergeant Skinner, though it would not be long before he would leave. Detective Gathers and I went to Sergeant Skinner, second-in-command of the detective division, and informed him that Detective Beck was about to arrest the wrong man. He abruptly stopped his work, stared at us and informed us that it was none of our business. It was as though he wondered what gave us the audacity to come into his office and tell him that a white officer was committing a felony. Of course, Sergeant Skinner still despised both George and me.

Sergeant Skinner's lack of professionalism proved detrimental to a number of black suspects. The Americana Motel case helped solidify my conviction that I would only arrest someone who I believed was the perpetrator. My morals and beliefs about doing the right thing allowed me to sleep at night.

Despite our plea, Sergeant Skinner did nothing, and Detective Beck arrested a man named Willie Waters and charged him with armed robbery. Waters maintained his innocence but was still indicted by the Charleston County grand jury and went on trial for armed robbery on June 4, 1970. He was convicted and sentenced by Judge Clarence Singletary to twenty-five years in prison.

Detective Gathers, Williams and I continued our investigation of multiple armed robberies in the Charleston County area. Our search continued until we had enough evidence to arrest the right man—the same person who we previously told Sergeant Skinner and Detective Beck had committed the robbery at the Americana Motel. We recovered evidence from the suspect's residence and arrested him for the series of robberies. The suspect confessed to all of the robberies, including the one at the Americana Motel. The suspect's confession exonerated Willie Waters.

Integrating the Charleston Police Force

On September 19, 1970, Governor Robert E. McNair issued a pardon on behalf of Willie Waters, and Waters was released from prison. Willie Waters suffered from injustice and discrimination simply because of the racist views and the political climate of the time. Unfortunately, these incidents of racism still occur, and there are still more Willie Waters waiting to be discovered. A short time after this, Chief Welch summoned Detective Beck into his office and told him that he better look for another job and gave him thirty days to leave. Detective Beck resigned from the police department and left South Carolina.

After a thirty-four-year career in law enforcement, I find it incomprehensible that with all the latest scientific technology law enforcement has at its disposal an innocent person can still be convicted of a crime. The public needs to look at the number of inmates who have been released from prison and exonerated. The reality is that they were only released because evidence surfaced that was withheld from defense lawyers and defendants during trial. I wrote about some of these travesties of justice in my book titled *From Segregation to Integration: The Making of a Black Police Officer*, which was released in 2001.

This book contains my observations concerning misconduct on the part of some police officers. I still stand by my writing then and now because there are documents in the records that substantiate my allegations. First, let me be clear that there were no other individual police officers in my department during my tour of duty who were tougher on crime and believed in law and order more than I do. My record in the department and the hundreds of cases that I assisted with and/or solved, coupled with the number of arrests I made in Charleston County, attest to this fact.

It has been my personal observation, opinion and experience that for an innocent person to be convicted of a crime he or she did not commit, one or more factors must occur: officers must perjure themselves, manufacture evidence, withhold evidence or misrepresent evidence due to incompetence or racial prejudice, or overzealous prosecutors must commit misconduct for their own political gains.

The majority of the police officers who serve this nation by placing their lives on the line twenty-four hours a day from the early days of law enforcement to the present are honest and above reproach. They need to be commended. I support them 100 percent. Therefore, I take the position that a police officer who is shown to be in violation of departmental policy, shows prejudice against a race of people or has a record of lying should be terminated for the good of the department, its fellow officers and its citizens.

There is no place for the "blue code of silence" during these tumultuous times. This is one of the reasons why turmoil continues between the police and its citizens. It does not matter how high up the ladder the problem reaches; it must be dealt with. During my entire career spent in the police department, I served no less than six police chiefs and two interim chiefs. No one is immune from being replaced, even a chief of police.

DURING THE 1960s, THERE were only three African American detectives on the Charleston County force, James L. Mikell, George H. Gathers and Jesse Williams. Later, I would be promoted to a detective and was transferred to the detective division. By 1972, I had investigated more than twenty-eight armed robberies of supermarkets, liquor stores and 7-Eleven stores in metropolitan Charleston County. Arrests were made in all of these cases, and the suspects were indicted by the grand jury. The defendants either pleaded guilty or were found guilty by a jury. Many of the suspects pleaded guilty when they realized the evidence against them was overwhelming.

Later in 1972, a memorandum went out seeking nominations for the 1972 Policeman of the Year award. Personnel with the local highway patrol and all police departments in Charleston, Berkley and Dorchester Counties were encouraged to submit the names of their candidates.

Chief Paul F. Hartline's memo advised the supervisors in the uniform and detective divisions to submit the most qualified candidate. Captain Richard F. Grassie, who was in charge of the detective division, told Lieutenant Michael Whatley that they had to check their records for the most qualified police officer. Lieutenant Whatley, my immediate supervisor, told Captain Grassie, "Tony, you don't have to look any further than Gene Frazier. No one in the department can match his record."

Captain Grassie was unaware that I was in the outer office when he told Whatley, "I am not going to recommend him for the Policeman of the Year Award."

Whatley told Grassie, "Tony, I am not recommending anyone beside Gene Frazier for the Policeman of the Year award. If you insist, we can take it to the chief."

My name was subsequently submitted by Captain Walter Gay and Lieutenant Whatley to Chief Hartline, despite Grassie's objections. Chief Hartline accompanied me to the ceremony. Detective Sergeant M. Dean

Powell from the city police department and Corporal F.R. Hollman from the South Carolina Highway Patrol were the other nominees. Both of the other officers were white. Sergeant Powell was considered the frontrunner; he was accompanied by Chief John Conroy.

The first time I remember hearing Chief Hartline laugh was when he saw Sergeant Powell and Chief Conroy start to stand just before my name was announced as the winner by Jesse Schultz, chairman of the Exchange Club. I was the first African American to receive the Policeman of the Year award in Charleston. Hartline was always the epitome of the no-nonsense drill sergeant, but on this day, he was tickled. It was out of character for him.

Although my record of accomplishments exceeded that of every detective in the division, I remained a detective corporal while white males came in the department later than me and were promoted over me. Some of these men came three years behind me and were supervised by me.

Jesse N. Williams

Jesse N. Williams was among the first group of African American men hired as police officers in the Charleston County Police Department. He was a straightforward person. He was deeply religious, and if something was not right, it offended him. He had a heart when it came to serving the underserved. He believed in looking out for his fellow men. It was hard for all of us to stomach the mistreatment of African Americans, but for Jessie, it was unbearable.

On a Friday in August 1966, Jesse and I were working the 3:00 to 11:00 p.m. shift. We were driving car number twenty-two, a marked 1965 Chevrolet. Around 6:30 p.m., the police radio dispatcher sent us to a disturbance at the Krispy Kreme on Rivers Avenue, near police headquarters. Krispy Kreme was where most of the police officers took their morning coffee-and-donut break. The disturbance involved a white male who apparently had too much alcohol to drink. His girlfriend assured us that she would take him home, and since no crime had been committed, we released him. Jesse and I checked back into service and informed the dispatcher of the girlfriend's assurance to take the subject home. Squad Sergeant Marlow overheard our decision to release the subject and instructed the dispatcher to tell us to lock him up. An obviously embarrassed dispatcher came back over the air and informed the sergeant that the man

Patrolman Jesse N. Williams.
Courtesy of family.

we released was white. Marlow came back on the radio and said that was okay.

Jesse was upset and said, "Did you hear that SOB saying 'nigger' over the radio? Wanting us to lock the man up if he was black, but it was okay to let him go since he was white?" This really got to Jesse. We let it go and continued doing our jobs as police officers, but sometimes it was hard. I thought about how I survived my tour in the army while stationed in Korea in 1953, and I was determined to survive the maze of injustice, discrimination and pain that I was forced to work through in the police department.

Jesse and I were also involved in what would become a major civil rights issue in Charleston. This issue centered on the hospital workers' strike that occurred in March 1969, when nurses, most of them women, at the Medical College Hospital walked off their jobs. Jesse and I, along with approximately eighteen white officers, were assembled behind the police headquarters on Pinehaven Drive. We were told that this was going to be a practice formation on crowd control. We were equipped with bayonets on M-1 rifles in case the city police department needed help with the strikers. The drill was going along just fine until Sergeant Reese Irwin, who was conducting the formation training substitute, made a derogatory comment. Jesse and I were understandably upset.

Jesse and I talked after we finished the exercises. I said, "Jesse, you know I served six years in the United States Army and received an honorable discharge as a Sergeant E-6, but there is nowhere in hell I will use a bayonet on black women—or any woman for that matter!"

Jesse and I went to see the operation bureau chief Paul Hartline and made a complaint. We were never used by the city police department, and nothing ever came of the complaint.

One day, Jesse said to me, "Frazier, I don't know how long I will stay with this department if this racial mess continues." He added, "I am talking with attorneys Michael O'Connell, Dale Cobb and Dan Bowling about employment with the county public defender office as an investigator."

I reminded Jesse of what Detective Mikell said to us before he left the department—that someone had to persevere on the job and help change the culture in the police department for African Americans. If Jesse decided to quit, I guess that left me to carry on. Jesse did resign from the county police department in 1974. He was hired as an investigator for the public defender's office and served for several years, until his death.

In the meantime, I kept busy. I secretly kept the late J. Arthur Brown, president of the local NAACP; the late senator Herbert U. Fielding; and the late reverend Cornelius Campbell, of the St. James Presbyterian Church on James Island, informed about the positions of local police departments on issues affecting African Americans.

Reverend Cornelius L. Campbell Jr. *Courtesy of Campbell family.*

JAMES OWENS JR.

May 10, 1968, is a day that I will never forget. That day has been etched into my heart, for it was marked by tragedy and heartbreak. Many of us were still mourning the death of our beloved Dr. Martin Luther King Jr., who was assassinated just a month earlier in Memphis, Tennessee. And then an event happened that was much closer to home.

On May 10, James Owens Jr., a fellow officer and close friend, and I were working the 3:00 p.m. to 11:00 p.m. shift. After we completed roll call, Jim and I walked to our assigned cruisers in the parking lot. I was assigned to unit number thirty-one, a 1967 Plymouth Fury. Jim was assigned to unit number twenty-six, a 1967 Chevrolet "crash wagon ambulance." During the 1950s and through the 1960s, there were no emergency medical services, so police officers had to transport the injured and the dead to the hospitals. Jim and I stood by our cruisers discussing where we were going to socialize after getting off duty. We decided on the Porgy and Bess Club on James Island.

After our decision, Jim abruptly changed the conversation. He said, "Gene, you know, every day we put on this uniform, gun and badge and

Patrolman James Owens Jr.
Courtesy of Owens family.

leave home not realizing that we might never return." The remark caught me off guard. Although Jim was serious about his job as a police officer, he was always a happy-go-lucky kind of guy. Jim had been on the force for close to two years, and I had been on the force for almost three years. I knew the dangers faced by police officers. I told Jim he was right, that we had to be careful and take life as it comes. Jim then drove off in his cruiser. I stood there for a moment wondering why he had made that statement. Then I got into my cruiser and checked 10-8, informing the dispatcher that I was in service.

Jim came on the force about a year before I lost my brother Jimmy, who died at just twenty-two as a result of pneumonia. It was devastating for me. I had an older brother, Sandy, who died in infancy before my birth, so Jimmy was the only brother I ever knew. Jim Owens proved to be a source of comfort for me during this trying time. I could call on Jim for anything.

Jim was a tall, striking man. He was married and had eight children. He was the type of person with whom anyone would feel comfortable. He was quick to laugh and was easy to get along with—unless you did something wrong. He was known in the community for being passionate in looking out for young people. Jim was also passionate about his favorite singer, Otis Redding. If you were riding with him and the radio was playing any of Otis's songs, you had to be quiet. Jim would move his head and body while swaying back and forth, smiling and singing with Otis. Jim was the only one who got a special assignment on Edisto Island. He was specifically asked by Chief Welch to look out for the chief's mother, who resided in the area.

The tragic events of May 10, 1968, began when Jim arrested a white man named Pye, who he knew in the Edisto area, for driving under the influence. Jim reported that he had Pye in the car and was told by the dispatcher that there was a wreck in his area involving a white female and a white male, and he needed to report to the accident scene. Jim told Pye that he could not release him at this time to drive. He was also unable to take him home, so he would have to take him to jail. Pye said, "OK."

When Jim arrived at the scene of the accident, he noted that the female was injured. The male was Wilkins C. Atkinson. Pye helped Jim load the female into the crash wagon. Jim transported Pye and Atkinson, along with the injured female, who Atkinson identified as his common-law wife, to the Charleston County Hospital emergency room to check her injuries.

Jim had not searched Atkinson or the female because they had not been placed under arrest. However, once at the hospital, Jim started asking Atkinson about the paperwork for the car so that he could write up the accident report. Pye later recalled that Atkinson became frigid and evasive. Jim was unable to determine if the car was owned or stolen and became suspicious of Atkinson's actions. He telephoned headquarters, and Detective Corporal Mickey Whatley told him to question Atkinson again, and if Atkinson did not answer the questions, to lock him up. When Atkinson continued to be evasive, Jim placed him under arrest.

Jim performed a search of Atkinson and, satisfied there was no weapon, placed him in the right rear bucket seat of the crash wagon. Pye, who was in the front seat next to Jim, testified that he noticed when they turned onto Calhoun Street just before reaching Rutledge Avenue, Atkinson reached down with a jerky movement. He came up with a gun. Atkinson shot Jim four times in the back of his head. Pye opened his door and rolled out onto the street. He watched the crash wagon roll into the bushes and stop. Atkinson got out and took off running.

Pye went back to the crash wagon and called the dispatcher and reported that a policeman was shot. The dispatcher responded by asking all officers to report in. Jim was the only one who did not report in. I knew it had to be Jim.

When I arrived at the hospital, the doctor was frantically trying to save Jim's life. However, after about five minutes of working on Jim, the doctor told the nurse to call it. I knew what that meant—my friend Jim was dead.

Jim's brother Nathaniel, who was a trainee at the time, arrived with his trainer, Patrol Officer Carroll Gordon. I received a call from Chief Welch to take Nathaniel home and inform the family about Jim's death. I was also to tell his family that the chief wanted them to call me if they needed anything, and I was to relay this information to his personal secretary, Marva Riddle, who would inform the chief. Nathaniel was in shock, and the family was devastated.

Former Solicitor Robert Wallace. *Courtesy of Robert Wallace.*

In the trial that followed four months later, Ninth Circuit solicitor Robert B. Wallace asked a jury for the death penalty. He attempted to convey Jim's impeccable character. Pye was the chief witness for the prosecution. He testified concerning the events before and after Jim's murder. He also testified about Jim's character and remarked that Jim treated everyone with respect. His testimony convicted Atkinson.

I respected Wallace for the way he handled Jim's case, but even before this case, he had already gained my respect and admiration. During the 1970s, defense attorneys would visit police headquarters to talk with detectives regarding their individual cases. However, the detective's supervisor would often refuse, referring them to the solicitor's office. One of the captains in charge of the detective's division, on at least one occasion, led defense attorneys to believe that the detectives did not want to talk to them. The truth is that we did not have the authority. The captain had the authority and did not want the detectives to talk with the defense attorney and, rather than saying so, would tell the defense attorney that it was the detective who did not want to talk.

Wallace's policy was to allow defense attorneys to speak to the detectives. He had no problem with detectives supplying the defense attorneys with statements, as long as the solicitor's office had the original statement. I was in agreement with his policy. I always based my statement on information obtained during my investigations so that there was nothing to hide. As a detective, it was my job to gather information during my investigation and present these facts to the solicitor's office, which would determine whether this body of information should be presented to the grand jury for an indictment against a suspect. If I gathered this information honestly and to the best of my ability, why would I want to hide this truth from the defense attorney? Are we not all on the same side—the side of justice? No one should want an innocent person convicted for a crime he or she did not commit.

Wallace realized that public defenders or defense attorneys often have a hard time speaking with police officers. For many defense attorneys, it was like trying to get through a brick wall. The term "justice is blind" should not only be displayed on the courtroom walls but also on the walls of every agency involved in the criminal justice system, including the walls of police departments and correctional facilities—from beginning to end.

On September 17, 1968, after deliberating for one hour and forty-six minutes, the jury of six men and six women announced that they had reached a verdict. Judge Louis Rosen was concerned about security in the courtroom and mentioned his concerns to Corporal Walter Gay. Corporal Gay assured him that security would be sufficient, as he had positioned me at the left entrance to the courtroom and Patrolman Richard Rouse at the right entrance. The judge looked around and appeared satisfied.

The clerk then stepped up and read the verdict: guilty of capital murder. At 7:00 p.m., Judge Rosen sentenced Wilkins C. Atkinson to die by electrocution and told him, "May God have mercy on your soul." The courtroom went quiet. You could hear a pin drop. It appeared that people were waiting to hear the clerk say something about a recommendation of mercy because Atkinson was white, but it never came.

I was the last one to leave the courtroom. Before I did, I paid homage to my friend James Owens by looking toward the ceiling and telling him that I was satisfied.

This was the first time in the history of South Carolina that a white man had been sentenced to death for the murder of a black man. The U.S. Supreme Court would later rule that the state's death penalty, as it was written, was unconstitutional. Thus, Atkinson's sentence was commuted to life in prison. He died in May 2010, after serving forty-two years behind bars.

James Owens III's tireless effort to honor his father in some way was realized fifty years after his father's murder. The state legislature directed the state department of transportation to place a sign on Calhoun Street near the site of the shooting, identifying the area as the Officer James Owens Memorial Intersection. The memorial was held in the park at the corner of

Eugene Frazier Sr., Fred Stroble and James Owens III at dedication for James Owens Jr. Memorial Intersection. *Courtesy of Geraldine F. Minter.*

Rutledge Avenue and Calhoun Street. It was a beautiful spring day. There were many people in attendance, including family, friends and other police officers. The memorial included the playing of bagpipes and honor guards.

State Senator Marlon Kimpson initiated the campaign to install the sign. About Jim, he said, "He may have been subjected to racial hostility because of his color, but he continued to serve despite those insults. And he made the ultimate sacrifice for his community." Fred Strobel and I were two of the speakers at the memorial. We were the last of the pioneers from the city and county police departments during the integration era, and now I am the sole pioneer. We were deeply moved by this dedication to our friend. I spoke about my personal relationship with Jim and the fact that he treated everyone with respect. I also remarked on Jim's assignment by Chief Welch to have Jim look out for his mother. Jim was so deserving of this honor. It took a long time, but the day that it arrived was special, and one that I will never forget. Jim would have been proud.

Integrating the Charleston Police Force

As early as 1973, there were rumors floating around in the department that the FBI was investigating the Charleston County Police Department for corruption. The charges included individuals taking payoffs from nightclubs for protection, allowing gambling and prostitution and selling liquor illegally. The reality of that investigation came to fruition on Wednesday, March 5, 1975, when a shockwave rolled through the police department. An announcement was made by the news that Charleston County Police chief Paul Hartline had been arrested by the FBI on federal extortion charges. Hartline and five members of his vice squad were indicted. Hartline pleaded guilty and was sentenced to a federal institution. Captain Walter Gay was appointed acting chief while the county manager and county council searched for a new chief.

Hartline's arrest was just one of a series of tragic events that would plague the department. Another occurred on November 15, 1974. I was sitting in my unmarked car on Morris Street next to Brooks Restaurant talking with an informant when an alert came over the police radio. The alert stated that there was an armed robbery in progress at Sam's Red & White Store on Folly and Camp Roads on James Island. Shots had been fired, and an officer was down. Detective Sergeant George Gathers was already on the scene when I arrived to find out the extent of this event. Patrolman William Cribb had been shot and died from several gunshot wounds fired by the robbers.

Sergeant Gathers and I were the senior veteran detectives in the department and had a record of success in solving homicides and robbery cases. Nonetheless, Detective Captain R.F. Grassie ignored our records and assigned two young, inexperienced detectives, Michael D. Boggs and Darrell Sanders, both of them white, as lead detectives on the case. Captain Grassie ordered Sergeant Gathers and me to turn over any evidence or information we received from our investigation.

On February 28, 1975, Captain Grassie called a meeting of all detectives assigned to the Cribb murder investigation at headquarters in the lecture room of the detectives' office. Those in attendance included representatives from the FBI; the Federal Bureau of Alcohol, Tobacco and Firearms (ATF); SLED; North Charleston Police Department; Charleston City Police Department; Sergeant Gathers; and me.

During the meeting, Captain Grassie made the statement that it had to be a black person largely due to the way Patrol Cribb was gunned down.

I told George that I was going to challenge Grassie—this was one black man who took exception to his opinion. I was about to stand up when Grassie asked if I had anything to say. George held me in the chair and told me

Grassie wanted us to say something so he could get us for insubordination. It took a lot to keep my cool that night because my emotions were tangled with the way he degraded all African Americans and my feelings over the loss of a dear friend. His statement was branded onto my brain.

People often ask why there are so many injustices against black people by police officers. Well, Grassie's comment is one of the reasons—because there were and are racists on police forces, and, too often, they are unchallenged. These statements breed a form of systemic racism that continues until other whites tell the people making such comments that they have to stop. They must let them know that their racist remarks will not be tolerated. When they stand up like that, they will make a difference in the fight against racism. Unfortunately, not one of the white officers from any of those departments or agencies said a word.

I discussed the unsolved murder of my friend William Cribb, whom I called Billy, in my book *From Segregation to Integration: The Making of a Black Policeman*.

Billy and I were friends growing up on James Island. I first met him at the Carolina Skyway Airport on James Island, located on Riverland Drive next to the King Solomon Lodge Hall on the Dill plantation. I was a teenager

Left: Officer William Cribb. *Courtesy of Captain Joyce Kephart.*

Right: William Cribb as a teenager at Skyway Airport on James Island. *Courtesy of Winifred Cribb.*

at the time, and Billy was younger. Billy was not just my friend, but he was also a fellow police officer, and I was distressed by his murder. I was also distressed because I knew that George Gathers and I were the most qualified to investigate the murder. We would have done everything we could to solve this case. However, we were not given the chance. Instead, inexperienced detectives were assigned the case. They were unable to solve the case, and it remains unsolved

I spent many hours with Patrolman Cribb's mother prior to her death. I will always remember her telling me, "Gene, I know racism was the reason my son's murder remains unsolved because you and George were not allowed to work the case." Because of my knowledge of the case, I totally agree with her.

EVENTUALLY, IN 1974, SERGEANT Gathers and I were able to strike back at the years of disrespect we had suffered due to the county's unwillingness to hire and promote black police officers. We filed a $1 million civil rights lawsuit against the Charleston County Police Department and Charleston County government. George and I were tired—bone tired—of the discriminatory ways we were treated. We were tired of hearing African Americans referred to as "niggers" and "dogs." It was time to make a difference because for far too long we had watched racism grow because of indifference.

I wondered what would have happened if one of the other white officers in that meeting had challenged Major Grassie about the way he referred to black people.

Would that have made a difference? George and I both knew that I would have been finished if I had challenged Grassie, but the same would not have happened to one of our white counterparts. Yet not one officer said a word. George and I had to walk a tightrope.

We watched our every move for two years. Sometimes after supervisory meetings I would explain the briefing to the men in my squad. I would then be told the instructions that I gave to the men were wrong. I learned to carry a mini tape recorder to every supervisory meeting to protect myself from false allegations. I still have many of those tapes today. Lieutenant Roddy Perry was the only person who knew I was taping these meetings. He kept me informed of any negative things being discussed concerning me.

In 1974, before our lawsuit went to trial, Detective Gathers and I were investigating the armed robbery of several supermarkets within the metropolitan Charleston County area. After several weeks of an intensive investigation, we arrested William Elrod, a white male, and four black males, Marvin Spell, George Moultrie, Bernard Fleming and George Denson. We confiscated two .38-caliber revolvers that were in the suspects' possession. Ballistic tests confirmed that one of the revolvers had been used in the murder of the owner of the grocery store in Columbia. The serial number on the second revolver revealed that it had belonged to the murder victim and was taken during the robbery. All information was turned over to the Columbia Police Department in the fifth judicial circuit. The five men were indicted for murder, armed robbery and unlawful use of a weapon.

In 1976, attorney Andrew Savage III, assistant solicitor to James C. Anders in the fifth judicial circuit, was put in charge of this case. Savage met with George and me at the Charleston County Police Department to prepare his case because we were the arresting and investigating officers in charge. Gathers and I were in the outer detective office when Savage went into Captain Grassie's office and asked to speak to us concerning the case. Grassie was unaware that Gathers and I were in the outer office when he asked Savage, "What you want to speak to those two for?" Andy Savage has never forgotten that day.

When this case went to trial, four of the men were convicted of armed robbery and sentenced to twenty-five years in prison; the fifth man was sentenced to life in prison. Savage wrote a letter to the chief of police (by then it was John H. Ball) thanking Detective George Gathers and me for our assistance in the case. In part, he wrote, "Cpl. Eugene Frazier and Sgt. George Gathers are true professionals; they are indeed a credit to their profession and particularly to the Charleston County Police Department. I can assure you they impressed our staff not only with their investigation but with their assistance in trial preparation and the appearance and demeanor as State's witnesses."

In 1976, following this case, George and I found ourselves dealing with our discrimination lawsuit. After our testimonies in the trial at the United States District Court for the District of South Carolina, Captain Richard F. Grassie admitted that as a white man born and raised in the South

Attorney Andrew J. Savage III.
Courtesy of Andrew J. Savage III.

during segregation, he used the word "nigger." He said he used it to refer to black people because using the word "nigger" was an accepted way of life for his community. The trial judge upheld the section of the suit dealing with the hiring, promotion and disrespect and ordered the county to implement a policy in reference to the hiring and the promotion of black officers. However, he dismissed our claim of monetary damage in the amount of $1 million without an explanation.

In 1980, Andrew Savage relocated to Charleston, where he joined the ninth circuit solicitor's office. A year later, he went into private practice in Charleston. He has been practicing ever since and is regarded as one of the best trial lawyers in South Carolina. Andy and I remain friends, and after I left the United States Marshal Service, I have worked as a private investigator on some of his cases.

Chief John H. Ball

John H. Ball was hired as chief of the Charleston County Police Department in 1975. At the time, the department was in a state of moral decay. The public had lost confidence in the department because of its history of corruption over the past two decades. The public really lost its trust after Chief of Police Paul Hartline and three members of his vice squad, along with Charleston County Council chairman James Price, vice chairman Claude Blanchard and members of county council were indicted by a federal grand jury on racketeering and corruption charges and sentenced to prison.

Ball, a tough, six-foot-four police chief from Jamestown, New York, let it be known from the start that he intended to build the Charleston County Police Department into a professional organization with integrity. He announced that those members who did not conform should seek employment elsewhere.

Ball knew he had to win the public's trust to accomplish his goals. One of the first of many changes he made was to create a written manual governing the department's standard operating procedures, including written communications, rules, regulations and directives. Ball also created an internal affairs unit to deal with allegations of misconduct and complaints involving police officers. He ordered all officers who served on the vice and narcotics section of the department, and members who had a cloud

Chief John H. Ball. *Courtesy of* Charleston Post and Courier.

of suspicion hanging over their heads prior to his arrival, to be polygraphed by SLED. Deputy Chief Walter Gay was given that assignment and saw that it was done. These tests forced the resignation of a high-ranking command officer and six other officers in the department. Their removal helped to alleviate the stigma of the remaining members of the vice squad and narcotics department.

Prior to Chief Ball's arrival, no African American could serve on the vice or narcotics squads. Members of the vice squad and the narcotics department reported directly to the chief. Ball's promotional policy would alleviate most of the problems that prevented African Americans from being promoted.

Chief Ball promoted me to detective sergeant (the same position as George Gathers), along with three white males in the uniform division.

There were 122 officers on the force, including 2 white females, 8 black males and no black females when Chief Ball assumed command. His recruitment program allowed me to find qualified African American candidates. I interviewed the first two African American females for employment, Cheryl Gadsden Byrd and Gwendolyn Frazier (no relation). Officer Byrd became the first female patrol corporal in the department, and Frazier became the first African American female in charge of the personnel division. Gwendolyn was already employed as a civilian at the police department when she was offered the position. However, she chose to decline the offer and remain a civilian. I also interviewed Robert Cochran from the Ravenel/Hollywood area and Nathaniel "Tanny" Smalls from the Edisto Island area. Robert Cochran would end up retiring from the police department after serving twenty-five distinguished years. I recommended both for employment. After passing the usual background investigation and physical and written examinations, they were immediately hired.

When Chief Ball left the department in 1979, there were 154 officers on the force. Of these, 16 were black, which doubled the number when he took command. During Chief Ball's last year of his four-year tenure as chief of police, the Charleston County Police Department attained a reputation of integrity and became one of the most professional police departments in the Southeast. We had applicants from other police departments throughout South Carolina, several states on the East Coast and even military men. Chief Ball never wavered. He accomplished the job he was hired to do and cleaned up corruption in Charleston County.

The political climate that existed before Chief Ball's tenure went underground while he was chief. However, after he left, it began to reemerge. Prior to his departure, Chief Ball began to venture into an area of law enforcement in the metropolitan Charleston area that threatened the lifestyles of certain politicians. I knew at least one high command staff officer in the department who encouraged certain members of the department to release any negative information on Ball to certain members in the political arena. However, this was to no avail.

Both Chief Ball and I lived on James Island. One day, he asked if I would come to his home. He thanked me for my support during his administration and especially during a meeting before county council in 1979. Although he did not say so, I suspected that Chief Ball was thinking about retiring from the department. Several days later, Chief Ball announced his resignation just as I had guessed. I hated to see him leave because he was a damn good police chief. He was one of the best chiefs I have ever worked for, alongside Chief Silas B. Welch and Chief Walter Gay. All three of these men had integrity above reproach.

Chief Ball wrote a number of letters of commendation about my work to County Manager Richard Black for solving a number of complicated murder cases. These cases included the murder investigation of Annette Lee Young with Detective Roddy Perry and my assistance with the Colleton County Sheriff's Office in solving the double homicides that resulted in the arrest of Sammie L. Butler. I was also recognized for the arrest of Sammie Butler's brother Horace Butler for kidnapping, rape and murder.

In one of Chief Ball's letters, he noted, "You are commended for your excellent performance of duty. Your intensive investigative work and apprehension of an individual…exemplify the finest traditions of police service. Your achievements in connection with this case are a credit to the profession and the Police department.…Congratulations on a truly fine performance." I was also named Policeman of the Month for the months of February and March 1976.

CHIEF LUTHER J. MOWERY

Luther J. Mowery was appointed chief of the Charleston County Police Department in 1980, after the retirement of Chief John H. Ball. He made many changes, including an order that all sergeants, regardless of their position or assignment, would wear uniforms and be issued marked patrol cars. They would also, with limited supervisory responsibility, answer and handle primary calls. This would be the first time in twelve years that I wore a uniform. At this time, I was a detective sergeant and third in command of the detectives' division.

Two homicides had recently occurred, and this left only two young, inexperienced detectives, Peter Megget and John Simpson, in the detectives' division to investigate the cases. Neither had ever investigated homicide, rape or robbery cases of this magnitude. It was unheard of for a homicide detective in uniform and in a marked patrol car to meet with informants or private citizens to discuss information of a confidential nature. As I observed Chief Mowery's reorganization of the department, I knew from my experience of seventeen years on the force, with fourteen of those years solving homicides and robberies, that those changes would not be successful. I advised the chief that his proposals would hamper our investigations. I thought they would put him—and the entire department—on a collision course with disaster.

When I told him this, he looked at me as though I did not know what I was talking about. It was then that I suspected his treatment of me and contempt for me had nothing to do with my qualifications but everything to do with my race. Because of this realization, I kept my distance and stayed away from political controversy. Chief Mowery promoted Thomas Dawson to captain and placed him in charge of the metro-narcotic division. Mowery also ordered everyone in the division to be polygraphed. This caused an uproar in the department. The controversy surrounding Chief Luther Mowery's leadership style became so chaotic that by August 26, 1980, just eight months after he was hired, the county manager fired him.

Mowery called me after he was fired to request that I intercede on his behalf. He wanted me to talk with the chairman of county council Lonnie Hamilton III, who was an African American. He knew Lonnie and I were friends. Mowery had promised Mr. Hamilton that he would create a promotion policy in the department that would be fair to everyone. However, that policy was never formulated. Thus, I never bothered to return his call.

Integrating the Charleston Police Force

Councilman Lonnie Hamilton III.
Courtesy of Hamilton family.

Lonnie Hamilton III was an educator in the 1960s, a time when no African Americans held seats in any position on Charleston County Council and white leaders did not listen to the needs and concerns of black people in the area. Mr. Hamilton saw the need and decided to run for a seat on county council. He pledged to represent everyone regardless of race, and in 1970, he won a seat on Charleston County Council, the first African American to hold this position. He went on to win reelection from 1970 to 1990. He served twice as chairman and once as vice-chairman. He also built a reputation as a man with integrity for his work on county council and other humanitarian efforts. Very few honest police officers trusted any county councilman besides Lonnie Hamilton during the years of 1970 through 1975.

One of my lasting memories of Lonnie Hamilton occurred during the tumultuous 1980s, after the termination of Chief Luther J. Mowery. Major Richard F. Grassie was trying to garner support from interim manager William "Billy" Kooperman for the chief of police position. After receiving no support from Mr. Kooperman, Grassie finally called Chairman Hamilton. He informed Chairman Hamilton that if Hamilton would allow him to become police chief, he would publicly apologize for all the offenses he had committed against black people over the years. Hamilton told Grassie that it was too late to apologize and that he would never support him for the chief of police position. Grassie never became chief of police.

I worked closely with Chairman Hamilton for many years. I always respected him, and I know he respected me. In February 1973, he wrote to congratulate me on my selection as the Exchange Club of Charleston's Policeman of the Year. He noted, "Living in history when policemen are constantly under attack for misconduct, it is very gratifying to know that we have men of your caliber watching over us as we sleep at night."

During these years, I was involved with a number of serious confrontations with armed suspects. A 1981 article in the *Evening Post* describes one of four such incidents:

Detective Sergeant Eugene Frazier Sr. standing by his unmarked car. *Courtesy of author.*

Sitting in his car with his gun jammed and with an armed man about to shoot him, Charleston County Det. Sgt. Eugene Frazier knew he had just a moment to act. He ruined the gunman's first shot by grabbing the gun through the open car window, and then flung open the car door, spinning the man around and causing a second shot to go wild. And sometime during this brief flurry of action that probably saved his life, Frazier said, "I did some praying."

Frazier escaped unharmed and a suspect was charged with trying to shoot him, and with an armed robbery that took place moments before the confrontation with Frazier.

In all of these incidents no suspects were hurt or killed. I give thanks to the Lord God Almighty, who I believe used me as an instrument to ensure justice was done.

Integrating the Charleston Police Force

Chief Walter Gay

The Charleston County manager once again appointed Walter Gay as acting chief of police following the firing of Chief Luther Mowery. This appointment was due to the recommendation of council chairman Lonnie Hamilton III. Later, Chief Gay was offered the position as permanent chief, and he accepted.

Chief Gay promoted me to the rank of lieutenant in August 1982, because I passed the promotion examination test and continued successfully handling murder and robbery cases. But I suspect it was also the result of Lonnie Hamilton's inquiry. The promotion resulted in my transfer to the uniform patrol division. I became a supervisor over the uniform division in the north area of Charleston. My duties included overseeing my squad and acting in the capacity of a patrol lieutenant.

Many police officers and citizens of Charleston County, including Chairman Hamilton and members of county council, who were familiar with my reputation and success as a detective wondered why I was transferred out of the detective division and placed as a commander in the uniform patrol division. The answer was that a white sergeant who did not have the investigative experience that I did was promoted to lieutenant and placed in charge of the detective division. I highly respected Chief Walter Gay, but there was no question in my mind that the command staff officers in the department did not want an African American in charge of the detective division.

Chief Gay had confided in Hamilton and me about his health. He told us that the doctor was concerned about his weak heart, and he should not be under stress. This was why he did not really want the chief position. He told me that he accepted the position because Mr. Hamilton asked him to and because of the respect he had for him. This was why I did not file another discrimination lawsuit.

Meanwhile, I still assisted certain members of the city police department detectives' division in reference to its investigations whenever they requested my help.

Chief Walter Gay. *Courtesy of Charleston Post and Courier.*

CHIEF REUBEN GREENBERG

John Conroy, chief of the City of Charleston Police Department, died in November 1981, and thirty-nine-year-old Reuben Greenberg was hired as chief in 1982.

Greenberg was a colorful character, and not just because he was the first African American police chief in the history of the city. The son of a black mother and a Russian Jewish immigrant father, he had converted to Judaism. He held a bachelor's degree in anthropology and master's degrees in public administration and city planning and graduated from the FBI Academy. He taught sociology, political science and criminal justice at major universities. He served as an urban police chief in Florida and was deputy director of the Florida Department of Law Enforcement when he was hired in Charleston. I was a uniform lieutenant with the Charleston County Police Department at the time.

Chief Reuben Greenberg. *Courtesy of Sarah Greenberg.*

In the summer months of 1983, J. Arthur Brown, who I had known all my life, called and asked if I could meet him at his residence on James Island. I agreed. There I saw Chief Greenberg sitting in his full-dress uniform. Mr. Brown introduced me to the chief.

After some political discussions, Mr. Brown asked if I would escort Greenberg around James Island and introduce him to the leaders and ministers in our community. I agreed to this. Reuben and I rode around James Island in my unmarked police cruiser, stopping at several homes in or near the Westchester subdivision. These homes included those of Gonzales Waddy, George Hughes, Thomas Johnson, Reverend Cornelius Campbell of St. James Presbyterian Church and Reverend Alex White of First Baptist Church, as well as several businesses along Folly Road.

Many African Americans were impressed with Chief Greenberg. He was the first African American police chief in Charleston, and African Americans were proud of this. They were also proud of the information received concerning his law enforcement successes in Texas, Florida and Georgia. He exuded confidence and did not back down. For African Americans in Charleston, this was unheard of, and they were optimistic and impressed with his behavior and demeanor. They were pleased that Mayor Riley had hired an African American as chief of police.

I met and interacted with Chief Greenberg on several occasions. The next time I met Greenberg was at the S & S Cafeteria on Highway 7 in the West Ashley area. He told me that I might want to work for him. He liked my style. He explained that he would be breaking up the good old boy system and he could bring me on the job with pay equivalent to a lieutenant, and in less than two years he would make me a captain. But I wanted to think about it.

I met with Chief Greenberg again two months later, thanked him and explained that I appreciated his offer but would stay with Charleston County. The offer was tempting, but I had already learned the political climate in the county, and I knew who to trust. If I joined his department, I would have to start over to learn the same things. It would have been exhausting, having to watch my back all the time until I found out who could be trusted. I would see Chief Greenberg from time until he got sick and retired. Years later, Sarah Greenberg, Chief Greenberg's wife, invited me to attend Reuben Greenberg's funeral as an honorary pall bearer, along with Deputy Chief Jerome Taylor and Chief Greg Mullen. It was a great honor.

1984 Cases

In 1984, I was involved in two important cases that could have been very difficult to solve. Both were concluded relatively easily, with suspects arrested, tried and convicted. I was a uniform lieutenant on April 20, 1984, when I responded to an alarm at the First Federal Bank on Savannah Highway. There had been a shootout, and during the exchange of gunfire, one of our uniform officers, Larry Smoak, was shot twice. He was able to return fire, killing one of the robbers, Anthony Rose. Two others escaped.

As a result of my investigation, I identified one of the gunmen as Benjamin Bellman, who I knew because I had previously arrested him for armed robbery. The FBI and county police officers surrounded the suspect's residence off Bennett Yard Road in North Charleston. I also knew his mother prior to this incident, so I knocked on the door that evening, and Mrs. Bellman answered. I explained why we were there. She told me her son Benjamin was in his bedroom, and she invited us inside.

Detective Chevalier Harris and I entered the residence and arrested Bellman without incident. We escorted him to our unmarked police car, and Detective Tom Anderson attempted to place the suspect in his cruiser. I told Anderson that Detective Harris and I would handle the suspect. We did not need his help. Anderson walked away visibly upset, mouthing racial slurs. The case was turned over to the FBI by Captain Grassie, since it had jurisdiction over bank robberies.

On October 29, 1984, I was a uniform lieutenant commander in charge of the 4:00 p.m. to midnight shift, working in the West Ashley area. The department received a report of a shooting that occurred on Hickory Street, behind the old post office in Avondale. I responded to the scene with a uniform patrolman to find a deceased sixteen-year-old female, who was identified as Lucia Aimar, sitting in the front passenger seat of a car. Ms. Aimar's boyfriend Eric Burn, also sixteen, was wounded.

I subsequently learned that the victim and her friend had been sitting in his car when a young black male walked up, pulled out a gun and demanded money. Burn did not have any money but offered the robber Ms. Aimar's purse, which contained five dollars. Ms. Aimar panicked and attempted to roll up the window as the gunman walked around to the passenger side of the vehicle. He forced the gun into the window and shot Lucy at point-blank range. He then shot her boyfriend. A massive search was conducted that night for the suspect, but he was not found. The investigation was turned over to the detectives under the supervision of Roddy Perry, and I returned to my regular duty.

I knew that the first forty-eight to seventy-two hours of a homicide investigation were critical, and I knew that Lieutenant Ronald "Roddy" Perry, who was now second in command of the detective division, would need detectives with a vast amount of experience, knowledge, expertise and reliable informants to solve the case. Roddy and I had been partners working on homicide cases for eight years.

We had solved most of the homicide cases in Charleston County in the 1970s and the 1980s. All of the murder cases that were assigned to me as case agent were solved and adjudicated in court during my career. After several days passed without any progress in the case, Lieutenant Perry asked me to meet with him. During the meeting, Perry asked if I would consider going on special assignment in plain clothes and pairing up with Detective Chevalier Harris, a veteran detective, to solve this case. I knew Harris's reputation as a smart, no-nonsense person who was highly capable of solving cases, so I was more than willing to work with him.

INTEGRATING THE CHARLESTON POLICE FORCE

Ronald "Roddy" Perry. *Courtesy of Perry family.*

I told Roddy that I would consider handling the murder investigation under certain conditions. First, he would have to clear it with Walter Gay. I would make decisions regarding the investigation, and I would report directly to Roddy and have no contact with Dawson. Roddy and I went to see Chief Gay, and he agreed to my requests. Detective Harris and I conducted an intensive investigation and, as a result of our interviews with witnesses and informants, accumulated enough information for probable cause to arrest a man named Earl Matthews on charges of murder, assault and armed robbery. Matthews lived in the city of Charleston.

On November 4, 1984, at approximately 12:30 a.m., Detective Chevalier Harris and I entered the home of Earl Matthews. Matthews's uncle directed us to the second floor, where Earl was in bed. I placed him under arrest for murder and armed robbery. I explained his rights under Miranda and asked him if he understood them. He said, "Yes."

Detective Harris and I escorted him to our unmarked police car. Detective Harris got in the driver's seat, and I got into the rear seat with Matthews. I asked him why he shot the girl. He said that he panicked. I asked him where the gun was. He said he used the pistol of another uncle, who lived in West Ashley. He added that after the shooting, he returned the gun and placed it in the bedroom drawer. I gave Detective Harris the signal to head to headquarters while I radioed Detective Sergeant Paul Hawkins. Hawkins was standing by with a search warrant at the uncle's residence with a team of detectives that included Detective Tom Anderson. I told Hawkins where the weapon was located.

When we arrived at headquarters, Detective Harris and I escorted Earl Matthews to the second floor and placed him in the interview room of the detectives' office. I briefed Lieutenant Perry on the status of the case. Detective Tom Anderson was in the room with Matthews when Detective Harris and I reentered the interview room. I told Anderson that I did not need him—that Detective Harris and I would conduct the interview of

Earl Matthews. I had no intention of solving the case for him to get the credit. Detective Anderson got angry and stalked out of the room. Later that night I overheard him say, "Those two think they know everything." Harris reduced Matthews's statement to written form. It was signed by Matthews and witnessed by Detective Harris and me. The file was then turned over to Lieutenant Perry. Anderson was assigned as the case agent to put the file together for court. I then returned to my normal duties as patrol lieutenant.

Earl Matthews went to trial in May 1985 for the murder and robbery of Lucia Aimar and assault with intent to kill Eric Burn. Ninth circuit judge Lawrence Richter presided. Solicitor Charlie Condon had previously served notice that he was seeking the death penalty in the case.

The trial lasted several days, with the solicitor calling a number of witnesses. Detective Harris and I testified concerning the investigation, arrest and confession of Earl Matthews. On May 13, the jury deliberated for four hours. It found Earl Matthews Jr. guilty of murder, armed robbery, assault with intent to kill and unlawful possession of a weapon. Judge Richter sentenced him to death for the murder, twenty-five years for armed robbery, twenty years for assault with intent to kill and one year for unlawful possession of a weapon, with the sentences to run consecutively. Earl Matthews was executed on November 7, 1997.

Before Earl Matthews died, he typed a letter of apology to the families involved and to teenagers to inspire them to choose a path different from his. A copy of the letter was given to me by his attorney, Michael P. O'Connell, as Earl included me in this distribution list. It was a powerful letter that I have distributed to many schools in the area. I also gave it to my daughter Geraldine, who shared it with many children in and around the Norfolk and Chesapeake, Virginia areas.

Earl Matthews was a young man who could have gone on to college and become successful. What went tragically wrong and how can society prevent this loss in the future? It would be many years later when my daughter Geraldine returned home that we discussed a way to present this story to encourage children to be the best that they can be. She met Joyce Maybin Nesmith, executive director of Beyond Our Walls (BOWs), at a mentor's appreciation dinner, and the two shared their passions. Later, the three of us teamed up and presented a PowerPoint program using this letter to encourage young people incarcerated at the juvenile detention center in Charleston. Some of them came in hesitantly at first. But it wasn't long before the twelve young men became captivated by a life so similar to their own. Many of them seemed to change during that presentation.

Integrating the Charleston Police Force

It was not a preaching sermon but a presentation by three people who wanted them to succeed. The last thing given to them was a "You Make a Difference" ribbon. My daughter and I would go on to do several programs of this nature hoping to inspire other children to make positive differences in their communities. On my birthday about twelve years ago, one of her students wrote a letter telling me what a difference Earl Matthews's letter made in his life. He would read that letter every day before he left for school for encouragement. Earl's apologetic letter could never bring Lucy back or heal the scars and broken hearts of Eric Burns, their families and friends, or this community. But the letter is making a difference in the lives of so many other young people who may have followed the destructive path that he took. One thing we know for certain is it does take all of us working together to make a difference in the lives of all children. It is true that "it takes a village to raise a child." We must all be that village.

The Making of a Serial Rapist and a Killer

Note: The following contains details of sexual abuse and violence. All of the victims' names and addresses have been changed to protect them and their families.

The month of June 1983 was hot and humid, with temperatures in the upper eighties. It seemed like another normal summer in Charleston. However, on June 23, a report came in of a rape and burglary case on James Island. Soon, it was followed by several other similar cases. The citizens of James Island were shaken and bewildered. For quite a while, the Charleston County Police Department was baffled. The reports resulted in the creation of a task force of officers in the Charleston County metropolitan area. The case drew the attention of many, including, eventually, me.

Elsie Manor, an eighteen-year-old, was alone in her apartment on James Island around 11:30 p.m. The day had been extremely hot. She was in her bedclothes and was about to get into bed, when she remembered that the dining room window was open. As she attempted to close it, someone grabbed her from behind and put her in a chokehold. A knife was placed against her cheek, and the assailant told her if she screamed, she would be killed. He forced her into the bedroom and ripped off her nightclothes. He raped and sodomized her. She said it seemed like hours passed while the intruder sexually abused her. She wondered whether she would live or die as he continued to threaten her with death. After the intruder finished, he tied her hands behind her back and took money from her wallet. He left through the open window in the rear of the apartment and disappeared into the night. Though her hands were tied, she managed to unlock the front door. She opened the door and screamed until a neighbor came to her rescue. The police were called, and they determined entry was gained through an open window. The only description the victim could give the police was that the intruder was a black male wearing a nylon stocking that covered his face. She said the intruder mumbled about someone named Boger.

Pat Kansas, a twenty-three-year-old female, was home alone on July 1. She lived in a three-bedroom, brick-veneer home in the Dairy subdivision of James Island. Her husband was working the 11:00 p.m. to 7:00 a.m. shift at one of the local shipyards. She was lying on her couch watching television in her underwear and bra at around 11:00 p.m., when she realized that someone was in the room. She attempted to sit up, but the intruder forced her back on the couch and placed a knife against her neck and told her if she screamed, he would kill her. He ripped her underwear and bra from her body, raped her and had her perform oral sex on him. After he finished, he told her not to move for five minutes or he would kill her. He left through the rear door and disappeared into the night. Police were called, but the victim was so upset that the only information she could give them was that the intruder was a black male with a nylon stocking covering his face and head.

Bobbie Jacks, a twenty-five-year-old female, was living in a duplex apartment on Brant Road on James Island. July 15 was another hot and humid night. There was no breeze blowing. All the windows in her apartment were raised. She was alone, and her boyfriend was in Florida for the month. Sometimes she had one of her friends spend the night with her, but tonight she was alone. It was 1:00 a.m., and she was lying on her bed naked. She said she enjoyed sleeping in the nude and liked to admire her body in a mirror hung on the bedroom wall. She was unaware of the man standing in the shadow of the door leading to her bedroom, watching her. She looked in the direction of the door and saw a man holding a knife. A nylon stocking covered his head and face. He was naked from the waist down. He grabbed her and forced her body on the bed. He placed the knife to her throat and said if she screamed, he would kill her. He forced her legs apart and raped and sodomized her. The intruder left through a rear door and disappeared into the night.

The police were called, but the victim was distraught. The only description she could give was that the intruder was a small black man with a nylon stocking covering his face. She was adamant about the report being kept secret. She feared that if her boyfriend found out that a black man had raped her, he would be unable to handle it because of his hatred of black people.

Camera Tombs, a twenty-two-year-old female, lived in a duplex apartment in the Legree subdivision of James Island. On August 17, she decided to go to bed at approximately 1:00 a.m. She had been drinking and felt a little intoxicated. She was recently divorced and lived alone. She was awakened by a man on top of her who was naked from the waist down. His face and head were covered by a nylon stocking. He pressed a knife against her throat. The intruder told her that if she screamed, he would kill her. He raped and sodomized her while she pleaded with him not to kill her. The intruder threatened her until he was finished. He turned her over on her stomach and tied her hands behind her back with shoestrings. She continued pleading for her life. The intruder told her that if she didn't make a sound for five minutes she would not be harmed. He took a wallet containing fifty dollars, credit cards and her driver's license and left through the open kitchen window, vanishing into the night. She went to the kitchen and managed to get one of the knives. She cut the ties around her hands and called the police. She could only describe the intruder as a short, slender-built black male.

Bernice Pole, a twenty-eight-year-old female, had just driven into the parking lot of a West Ashley shopping center on September 7. It was late in the evening. She was unaware of a man standing in the shadows watching her as she parked. She exited the car and was grabbed from behind by a man wielding a knife. He placed the knife to her throat and told her not to scream or she would be killed. He forced her into bushes next to the shopping center and raped her. He took her pocketbook with $100 and vanished into the night. The police were called. The victim said that her attacker was a slender-built black male, about five-foot-four, with a nylon stocking covering his face.

Belinda McKee, a thirty-three-year-old female who lived on Helen Street behind Barkley Middle School on James Island, was found by her son on the kitchen floor with stab wounds on September 11. An autopsy revealed that she had been raped. She bled to death from the stab wounds. Her son reported that four guns were taken during the burglary and murder. An investigation revealed that entry was gained into the residence by prying open a kitchen window. There were no known witnesses to the crime.

At midnight on September 23, Verna Tradd, a thirty-year-old female who had just completed an eight-hour shift at one of the local hospitals, would be the next victim. Her car was parked across the street from the hospital in a parking garage. She didn't notice the man standing in the shadows behind her until she opened the door. The man placed a revolver to her head, got into her car and forced her to drive thirty miles from Charleston into Dorchester County. He instructed her to drive to a wooded area, where he raped her and then robbed her of $200. He forced her into the trunk of the car at gunpoint and drove back to Charleston, where he abandoned the car on the east side of the city. A concerned citizen heard her cry for help and notified the police. The victim described her abductor as a twenty-two-year-old, dark-skinned black male, slender build, about five-foot-four and about 135 pounds. During the rape, Tradd said her attacker kept talking about someone name Boger.

Clarie Henry, a twenty-four-year-old female who lived in a trailer park on Conyers Street, returned home from a party around 2:00 a.m. on October 12. She unlocked the door and went inside. Her husband was in the U.S. Navy and was at sea. She took off her clothes and entered the shower. She said she had a strange feeling that something was wrong, but nothing seemed out of place. She shrugged it off and dried off. She stated that she lay down on her bed in the nude. The trailer was warm. The only light in the trailer was from the television set she was watching. She felt strange, as if someone was watching her. She looked toward her door in time to see a man naked from the waist down with a knife in his hand. He rushed over and pushed her back down on the bed. He placed the knife against her throat and told her if she screamed, he would kill her. He made her perform oral sex on him and then raped her. He told her if she tried to escape, he would kill her.

The intruder made her lie down beside him for approximately thirty minutes, threatening her and saying something about someone named Boger. She did not understand. Boger, he said, wanted him to kill her. He got between her legs and performed oral sex on her, and after finishing he began sucking her breast. She begged him to let her use the bathroom, while assuring him that there were no clothes in the bathroom. He looked satisfied. He told her to hurry up. She closed the door, flushed the commode and wrapped a towel around her body. She opened the small bathroom window, crawled through it and ran to her neighbor's house. She banged on the door and told them what happened. This action probably saved her life. The man had vanished into the night by the time the police arrived. Henry described the rapist as a dark-skinned black male with short hair, twenty-two years of age, five-foot-four and weighing 135 pounds.

Integrating the Charleston Police Force

Tara Gotis, a twenty-five-year-old female and a nurse at one of the local hospitals, got off duty at midnight on November 8. She was last seen entering the parking garage where her car was parked. She vanished without a trace and was reported missing the morning of November 9. Her car was found several days later in a West Ashley shopping center. There were no clues as to what happened. Deer hunters in Dorchester County, thirty miles from Charleston, discovered Ms. Gotis's body on December 2. An investigation by police and the medical examiner revealed that the victim had been raped and then shot in the head at point-blank range.

By this time, detectives investigating the cases—over a six-month period—were increasingly frustrated. Even after months of investigation, they were unable to come up with any leads. The young detectives assigned to the case did not have the experience and expertise to handle cases of this magnitude and should not have been given the assignments. They also had no standard operating procedures from which to work. For example, an informer and a concerned citizen called the detectives and gave the names of four suspects they believed were involved in the rapes and burglaries. All of the men were at least five-foot-ten and up to six-foot-one, light-skinned and 165 pounds. These men should have been eliminated within hours of receiving the information, but they weren't.

All of the victims in these cases were adamant about height, weight, age and complexion. Yet the detectives spent weeks—even months—before eliminating these men. Major Grassie relieved these detectives from the case and sent them to other duties, saying they did not know what the hell they were doing. I did not blame them. These men had never been involved in a homicide investigation. Neither was their supervisor, who had little or no experience in a homicide investigation at that time. A task force was formed with officers from the entire local jurisdiction, even SLED, but despite all of their experience, no information developed in reference to a suspect.

I was a uniform lieutenant at the time. Major Grassie knew my record and accomplishments in homicide investigations. However, he never asked for my help. Meanwhile, pressure was increasing from the public. They wanted to know what the police were doing to apprehend the burglar and rapist. It was seven months since the first report, and the police had made no progress in the cases. Two of the victims were murdered. One barely escaped with her life. I believed it was just a matter of time before the rapist struck again. He was gaining more confidence in himself and escalating his criminal activity. During my tenure as a detective, I attended several courses conducted by the FBI. One of the courses was titled Profile of a Serial Rapist. It helped prepare me for this case.

Lieutenant Roddy Perry was second in command of the new task force. Roddy and I had worked as partners for eight years on homicide cases. He went to Chief Gay and then Major Grassie and informed them that if they wanted these cases solved, I should be placed on special assignment. He added that he knew of no one in homicide who had the expertise that I possessed. Grassie reluctantly gave in to Perry's request and the pressure from the public. He placed me on special assignment in plain clothes and in charge of the investigation.

I sat down with Lieutenant Perry and discussed each case. I was already familiar with most of the facts because I oversaw the uniform officers responding to the original complaints and signed off on their paperwork. I concluded from information given by the victims that the suspect was a black male, five-foot-four, weighing about 135 pounds, twenty to twenty-two years old, dark skinned with short hair. All of the burglaries except one occurred on James Island, so my investigation was focused there. No one could recall seeing a suspicious black male or a strange car in the community during the time these crimes were committed. The way in which the burglar managed to vanish without a trace suggested that he lived on the island. He probably did not own a car. I considered that the suspect either lived or worked in Dorchester County at one time. This would be consistent with the two victims who were forced to drive there. He appeared to know exactly where he was going. Many of the victims did not want to talk about their rapes, but all agreed that he was very potent and had a lot of sexual drive.

This suggested to me that the suspect was not married. I guessed that he lived alone or with relatives and probably would not be missed during his movements. He may not have a job. I was convinced that the same person committed every one of these crimes based on the fact that the burglar used identical methods during each crime. Lieutenant Roddy agreed with my evaluation of these cases. Because of our experience together, he and I had a good working relationship. I told him there was enough information available that convinced me this rapist had a history of assault on women. Detective Chevalier Harris and SLED agent Walter Mitchell were teamed up, and Roddy and I teamed up to continue the investigation. We selected one hundred names of black males between the ages of twenty to twenty-five who fit the description of the suspect, who had been arrested and who had a history of using a knife or a revolver in and around the Charleston metropolitan area. Photographs were shown to each victim, but they were unable to identify any of the photographs as the rapist. Each man was interviewed and cleared.

Our attention then focused on juvenile offenders matching the characteristics of the suspects who would now be adults. Roddy and I, along with Detective Harris and Agent Mitchell, began the tedious task of eliminating dozens of men who fit the suspect's description. We cleared seventy-five men. As we reached the seventy-sixth, the name Charles Edward Blake Jr. surfaced. I recognized him as the stepson of a cousin of mine. His mother was from Dorchester County. She had divorced her husband, Charles Blake Sr., and married my cousin and moved to James Island.

He fit the description of the suspect. Lieutenant Roddy Perry recalled arresting Charles E. Blake for attempted rape using a knife.

I told Lieutenant Perry, Detective Harris and Agent Walter Mitchell that Charles Blake was our man. He lived alone in an apartment on James Island, just two blocks from where two of the victims lived. He also lived within two miles of all of the victims' homes on the island. He did not have a job but attended a technical training school on Meeting Street Road between four and seven o'clock at night. He would have been available during the hours when the rapes and murders were committed. He was familiar with the area in Dorchester County where the women were forced to drive.

I suggested to Lieutenant Perry that he check for any evidence received from our lab technician at all crime scenes. He should also check the city police laboratory for any evidence taken from the victims' cars during the rape and robbery in Dorchester County.

Detective Harris, Agent Mitchell and I drove to Dorchester County and conducted some background investigation on Charles Blake. The investigations revealed that Blake came from a broken home and was a troublesome young boy in his school and neighborhood. He also had some problems communicating with other youth. The neighbors in the community where the Blake family lived before they moved to James Island thought that he was strange. They did not trust him around their daughters.

The investigation also revealed that Blake's father was a child abuser before he abandoned the family. When I returned to police headquarters, Lieutenant Perry was waiting for me. He informed me that among the evidence in the city police department's crime lab, there was a fingerprint taken from the trunk of Verna Tradd's car. The fingerprint was compared with the known fingerprint of Charles Edward Blake Jr. An expert said it was a match. A search warrant was executed on the trailer Blake now shared with a roommate in North Charleston. Blake was not present during the search. The team recovered a wallet and an ID taken from a victim during a burglary, confirming that Charles Edward Blake was our man.

A warrant was drawn on Charles E. Blake for the kidnapping of Ms. Tradd. On Friday, November 17, 1983, Lieutenant Roddy Perry, Detective Chevalier Harris, Agent Walter Mitchel and I set up surveillance on Blake's apartment on James Island. Surveillance was also set up on the trailer in North Charleston. On Saturday morning at 6:30 a.m., the suspect returned home and was taken into custody by Detective Harris and me without incident. He was taken to county police headquarters and placed in the interview room.

Detective Harris and I sat with Blake, and I advised him of his constitutional rights. He said he understood them. I asked him if he wanted a lawyer. He said he had done nothing that would require a lawyer.

I asked Blake if he knew who I was besides being a police officer. He said he understood that his stepfather and I were cousins. I told Blake that Detective Harris and I were investigating several burglaries and rapes and had reason to believe that he was involved. He denied any involvement or knowledge concerning the crimes. After questioning him for some time, I decided to drop what I thought should have been a bombshell on him. I placed before him the wallet, ID, credit card and driver's license taken from one of the victims that had been found in his trailer. He said he knew nothing about those items, but they might belong to his roommate. He seemed at times to be out in space. I must admit that Blake was not easily intimidated. It seemed as if what I said to him passed by without him registering it.

This continued for a couple of hours. When I thought he was worn out and tired and I had his attention, I told him that he was a "damned rapist and a killer." I told him that he left his fingerprint on the car of the woman he raped in Dorchester County. Blake stared at Detective Harris and me as though he was looking through us and said, "I guess I must have done those things, but Boger told me to do it." Boger? I asked Blake who Boger was. He said Boger was the person who tells him when to rape and kill.

He was referring to some supernatural power that took control of him. Blake said he moved out of his mother and stepfather's home on Riverland Drive to the one-bedroom duplex apartment on Chesser Drive in James Island. He stated that in May 1983, he began hearing a voice telling him he needed sex and to get it even if he had to rape someone.

He finally gave in to Boger and began to search for women alone in their apartments. He walked to numerous apartments and looked through windows. Sometimes he would knock on a door and ask for a fictitious person who he knew did not live there. He would check to see if the women lived alone. He watched the apartments for several days to see when the women would be alone. Blake began to tell us bits and pieces of what happened. I stopped the interview and informed Lieutenant Perry that we may have a problem with Blake's confession. But there was no question in my mind that Blake was our rapist and killer. I suggested to Lieutenant Perry that Dr. Gilbert Bradham, a medical doctor and a noted hypnotist, should be consulted.

Dr. Bradham had been instrumental in assisting us during several prior homicide investigations. I recalled one case where a female was attacked and beaten so savagely that she blocked out all memory of the attack, including the suspect. Through hypnosis, Dr. Bradham was able to have the victim relive the ordeal and identify the suspect. Dr. Bradham placed Blake in a hypnotic trance while Harris and I watched. I questioned Blake concerning every case of rape and murder during the eight-month period. Blake confessed to every case, confirming in detail all of the victims' statements, especially those four victims who stated that the suspect said Boger told him to rape and kill.

After the statements were taken down in written form, witnessed and signed, I asked Charles Blake if he would take us to those apartments where his victims lived. He took us to each house and apartment, and when he was finished, we realized there were four additional apartments on which we had no reports. Blake was adamant about raping those four women and described each one. The women were contacted and admitted being raped but said they did not report them because they did not want their husbands to know.

Charles E. Blake Jr. appeared in the Charleston County Court of General Sessions on eighteen charges, including burglary and one count of murder. The issue of an insanity plea was brought up, but the judge ruled against it. Therefore, Blake pleaded guilty and was sentenced to five life sentences in lieu of the death penalty and under agreement with Charles Condon of the ninth judicial circuit court. He also received an additional 245 years to run consecutive to one another.

On June 18, 1984, Blake appeared in the first judicial circuit court in Summerville, South Carolina, before first circuit judge John Hamilton Smith, for the crimes committed in Dorchester County. Solicitor Joseph Mizzell reluctantly accepted Charles Blake's guilty plea in lieu of going after the death penalty. He cited problems with the evidence in his case. He said that even though the victim was raped in Dorchester County, detectives were not called in on the case until Blake had obtained a lawyer. He believed that by that time it would have been useless to question him. (During the original interview with Blake, I had suggested to Lieutenant Perry that we should call the Dorchester County sheriff detectives in on the investigation. Major Grassie refused and told Lieutenant Perry that he made the decision when to call an outside agency in reference to the case. We left it there.) Judge Smith sentenced Charles Edward Blake to two life sentences and three thirty-year sentences, all to run consecutive to one another. He told Blake that he hoped to God that he would never see the light of day in this state as a free man.

In March 1986, Sergeant George Gathers and I sat down and discussed the future of African Americans regarding continued racial discrimination within the department. He said to me, "Frazier, it is up to you now to keep fighting for what you believe in. This old warrior is tired. I've been on the force for thirty-nine years. It is time for me to go."

I said to him, "Don't forget you are still one of the pioneers. I will always remember you and James Mikell for all your support and guidance."

George retired in 1986. I could see the stress in his face and fatigue over his body. He died six months after retiring. I felt like I was alone in the world after his passing. But somehow, I continued the fight. I began focusing on the promotion of Detective Chevalier Harris.

As a uniform lieutenant in 1986, my assistance was requested again in the detective division by the assistant chief, Major D.M. Boggs. A homicide occurred in North Charleston between Dorchester and Meeting Streets near Pinehaven Shopping Center. I walked across the railroad track to where the victim was lying. I immediately recognized the victim as Shirley Mae Mack, a black female who was a waitress at the Alex's Restaurant on Dorchester Road. The crime scene was located a short distance from the restaurant. She was friendly to many of the customers, including police officers.

The investigation led to Frank Middleton, an inmate who had escaped from the South Carolina Department of Corrections. Middleton had been serving sentences for an armed robbery and assault that occurred in Charleston County when he escaped from a prison work gang.

Frank Middleton confessed to the murder and rape of Shirley Mae Mack and the rape and murder of Beverly Gardner of North Charleston when he was arrested. Middleton said he was looking for women to rape. He said he knew Ms. Mack worked for Alex's Restaurant, and he followed her twice and knew the route she took to get home. On this particular night, he waited near the railroad track by the building and overpowered her. He was found guilty by a jury and sentenced to death. He was executed on November 22, 1996. Not long after the Middleton case, in June 1986, Chief Walter Gay retired. He died shortly after his retirement.

CHIEF WILLIAM J. SIDORAN

In July 1986, Charleston County administrator W.C. Furtwangler, under the direction of Charleston County Council, hired William Jack Sidoran as chief of the Charleston County Police Department to replace Chief Walter Gay. Morale was once again low. There was a power struggle in the department between command staff officers, and the hiring and promotion of African Americans had once again come to a complete stop.

Thomas Dawson had joined the department three years after me. He was a white man who left the department for a time and later rejoined it. By 1988, he was a major, and I was still a lieutenant. Many in the department and community were asking what was wrong with the promotion policy pertaining to African Americans.

Chief Sidoran had promised county council members, including the chairman, Lonnie Hamilton III, that under his reorganization, the plans for the department would include instituting a promotional policy that was fair to everyone regardless of race. Chief Sidoran approached me in the Union Heights area of North Charleston in August 1987 for a meeting and asked me the names of those white officers in the department who held the rank of sergeant, lieutenant, captain and major and had shown racial prejudice toward African Americans.

Lonnie Hamilton had advised him to talk with me about the racism and discrimination that existed in the department. Sidoran also felt that I could help him because I was the oldest black officer on the force, had achieved

Chief William J. Sidoran. *Courtesy of* Charleston Post and Courier.

the rank of lieutenant and was outspoken on issues. Sidoran assured me that the information I gave him would remain confidential. I told him I had no problem with him using my name because what I had to say was common knowledge. There were tape recordings, written department memorandums, statements, depositions, court records and cases adjudicated in court that substantiated my statements. I had no problem making any of my charges in the presence of these men.

The promotional process was soon completed, and after reviewing the list of men promoted, I was bewildered, disgusted and disillusioned. Thirteen officers were promoted but not a single African American. Most of the men who were promoted were those I had named to Chief Sidoran—the same men who had shown racial attitudes toward African American officers. Chief Sidoran did not promote any of the black command staff officers who were well qualified and had integrity. I wrote a three-page letter of complaints after reviewing the list of those men who were promoted.

PATROLMAN WILLIE ROBINSON WAS another young African American who joined the Charleston County Police Department after two years of outstanding service in the U.S. Army as a military policeman. He was assigned to my fifteen-man squad in 1983. During a three-year period, I noticed that Patrolman Robinson was one of those ambitious young men who wanted to succeed in his job. Every task he was assigned was accomplished with a high degree of proficiency. His public appearance was impeccable and consisted of tailored uniforms, shined shoes and a crew cut military hairstyle. His job performance was above average. He topped everyone in the squad. The department took notice and selected Robinson as one of two men and a female pictured on a recruiting poster representing the police department. However, when Robinson became eligible for promotion, he was passed over for white officers with far fewer qualifications.

White officers continued to be promoted over blacks with all kinds of dubious excuses. During Robinson's promotional board review, I read the list of the potential candidates' records. I also observed and listened to them as they appeared for their oral reviews. There were about sixteen board members, and all were white except me and one other. All of the board members voted along racial lines except Major Boggs, Lieutenant Perry, Captain James Atchison, Lieutenant Hawkins and Lieutenant Sexton. The one African American captain on the review board was no help—he voted with the whites.

Integrating the Charleston Police Force

Left to right: Patrolman Grady Brown, Patrolman L.F. Brown, Patorlman W. Robinson and Sergeant E. Sweat. *Courtesy of Willie Robinson.*

It was the same voting tactic that was used against Detective Chevalier Harris and other black candidates. It made me sick and disgusted. I complained to Major Boggs, the deputy chief and chairman of the promotional board. He agreed with me and went to Chief Sidoran. The chief listened to my complaint but refused to expand the number of candidates from eleven to twelve. This meant no blacks would be promoted. Thirteen white officers were promoted and not a single black officer. Detectives Harris and Robinson were two of the men who prompted me to write the three-page, blistering letter of complaint to Chief Sidoran concerning his promotional policy. I believe Boggs speaking out on this injustice contributed to Boggs's termination. I also believe that speaking out on racial discrimination issues was when I began being considered a threat to the county police department.

My letter was dated September 17, 1987, and was sent through the chain of command to Chief Sidoran, requesting permission to be excused from the actual promotional ceremony. I was extremely upset and went on to explain my displeasure with him and his command staff, acknowledging that there were no African American officers promoted, the promotions went to white officers whose jacket files contained many disciplinary actions and the lone African American captain in the department stood by silently throughout all of my complaints and did nothing to help the rest of the African American police officers who were being treated unfairly.

Detective Harris and I had a number of discussions in 1988 in reference to continuing racial discrimination in the department and Chief Sidoran's failure to take appropriate actions to end the practice. Subsequently, Detective Harris, through his attorney, filed a discrimination lawsuit against the Charleston County Police Department and Chief Sidoran. Detective Harris also filed a complaint in a letter dated July 27, 1988, to Chief Sidoran, accusing Captain E.S. Whitlock and Sergeant Tom Anderson of racial harassment and outlined the reasons. A copy was sent to the director of personnel, attorney William Runyon and the South Carolina Human Affairs Commission in Columbia. After reviewing the complaint, the S.C. Human Affairs Commission agreed with us, and the case was forwarded to federal district court in Charleston.

I gave a deposition in Detective Harris's lawsuit at the law office of Young, Clement, Rivers and Tisdale. The lawyers for Charleston County, after hearing part of my testimony, postponed my deposition and took depositions from others. However, prior to the trial in 1990, in the United States federal district court in Charleston, the attorney for Charleston County settled out of court with Detective Harris for an unspecified amount of money. Morale within the department was again at an all-time low in April 1988—even lower than when Sidoran was appointed chief.

The philosophies of the white command staff officers regarding racial discrimination forced county manager Ed Fava to read a statement to the entire command staff in a meeting at Trident Technical College in October 1988. Fava stated, "If the department did not have a black candidate qualified to be promoted to the rank of sergeant, the county would go outside the department to find a qualified black candidate." Detective Harris was subsequently promoted to sergeant.

THE YEAR 1988 ALSO saw an increase in crime in Union Heights, an unincorporated area of North Charleston. Crime was running rampant, and the citizens were afraid to be in public areas at night. Chief Sidoran, at the insistence of council chairman Lonnie Hamilton III, ordered Captain James Atchison, my immediate supervisor, to have me draw up a plan of action to deal with the problems in Union Heights.

Integrating the Charleston Police Force

At a Charleston County Council meeting, Chairman Lonnie Hamilton said the known enforcer should be called in to fight crime in the Union Heights area. He said, "people who frequent the area respect Frazier who's been effective in fighting crime in the area in the past." I handpicked a squad of six men from the officers working the north district. The squad reduced crime to a point where the people in the community were able to sit on their porches and walk the streets without fear. This happened within three months by using highly visible, aggressive police tactics. The tactics included officers working from 6:00 p.m. to 2:00 a.m. Prostitution, drug sales and other street crimes on Spruill Avenue and in the Union Heights area came to a halt. I received recognition from the community through a letter from Reverend Ed. McClain, minister of the Calvary Baptist Church, and signed by Secretary Jacqueline F. Hill of the Union Heights Organization. In 1988, for my work in Union Heights, I received the Policeman of the Year award for the second time from the National Exchange Club.

Chief Sidoran was invited to accompany me in October 1989 to accept the Policeman of the Year award, but he did not attend. My immediate supervisor, Captain James Atchinson, accompanied me. I had observed and scrutinized Chief Sidoran's philosophies by this time, and I realized that he was traveling on the same collision course with diaster that I had cautioned him about in regards to Chief Mowery. I had cautioned Chief Sidoran about those same command staff officers who had surrounded Chief Mowery. This group of officers eventually became Mowery's demise. Chief Sidoran completely ignored my advice, and these same men I advised him against were promoted.

The problems became especially noticable when Chief Sidoran terminated Major D.L. Boggs and made Thomas Dawson his assistant chief. I had supported Major Boggs at council meetings, and Dawson was one of the men I had advised the chief against promoting. Chief Sidoran's and Major Dawson's attitudes toward me became apparent following my letter on September 17, 1987. The letter stated my concern that retaliation was being planned against me because of my stand on racial issues in the department. Sidoran's promotion of Dawson to assistant chief spoke volumes about his credibility and the promise he had made to Lonnie Hamilton, the other county council members and me. Dawson's promotion also made clear Sidoran's views about a fair promotional policy.

In a meeting held on April 5, 1988, Charleston County Council approved the creation of a special interview committee including all members of county council. They would hear all police department employees who wished to comment on the department and the problems we faced. I addressed the county council's interview committee on May 16, 1988. I believe that what I told the full committee was a shock to some but not to others. It is now a matter of record. I told council that although Major Boggs had been the subject of much criticism, he wasn't the problem; Chief Sidoran and Major Thomas Dawson's leadership was the problem, and it kept the department in chaos. Based on my twenty-two years of experience in the department, and my knowledge of the men, I explained that Chief Sidoran was the number one problem. Council member Dr. Charles Wallace asked if I had the authority, how would I handle the problem. I said the first order of business would be to terminate Chief Sidoran, appoint Major Boggs as chief of police, remove Major Dawson to a lesser role and appoint another major as Boggs's assistant. Police officers in the department speculated that I would be terminated next, but Boggs received another position equivalent to a major in county government. This resulted in no retaliation against me or any other police officer.

The history of discrimination in the department resulted in several young, educated African American men and women leaving the Charleston County Police Department/Sheriff's Office from the 1970s through 2005. The reason for their departures was the continuing racial discrimination policy regarding promotions. Some of these men and women were:

- Detective Clayton Jones, who joined Naval Criminal Investigative Services (NCIS) and retired as a supervisor after twenty years
- Detective Amos Jones, with whom I partnered during the 1970s. He later formed a successful private investigative business in Columbia
- Detective Bernard Blaney, who returned to his former job as a schoolteacher
- Victor Hill, a young protégé of mine, who was a deputy with the Charleston County Sheriff Office. He was terminated from the department for some of the same reasons as many of the other African American males. Eventually, he moved to Georgia, where in 2005, he was elected Clayton County's first African American sheriff. He is now in his third term as sheriff. Hill has been recognized all over the United States and in many foreign countries, including Israel.

Integrating the Charleston Police Force

Above: Sheriff Victor Hill with Lieutenant Eugene Frazier Sr. *Courtesy of Victor Hill.*

Left: Sheriff Victor Hill. *Courtesy of Victor Hill.*

Charleston County Police / Sheriff's Office

- Sergeant Angela S. Palmer, who enjoyed a fine reputation in the department for many years. However, she ran up against the problem of the department's promotional policies, and after years of obstacles and discrimination, she retired.

Angela Palmer described her career this way: "Following graduation from James Island High School, I entered the United States Air Force and rose to the rank of sergeant. I was assigned as assistant flight sergeant of a team of twelve. Additionally, I was assigned as immediate supervisor to an average of four subordinates and directed LE flight operations during normal and emergency conditions. I was also in charge of monitoring personnel proficiency, conducting training, maintaining schedules for daily work assignments and approving leave requests for training and personnel data."

She continued, "I was hired as a deputy with the Charleston County Sheriff's Office in January 1993. I was assigned to the uniform patrol division and responded to calls for service, performed initial investigations, performed district patrol and traffic stops for violations of traffic laws and other services as required after training. As a master deputy, I was assigned to the Ceasefire Task Force under the Federal Bureau of Alcohol, Tobacco, and Firearms and Explosives. This task force worked with local law enforcement departments and adopted violent-weapons-violation cases and prepared these cases to be prosecuted in federal court.

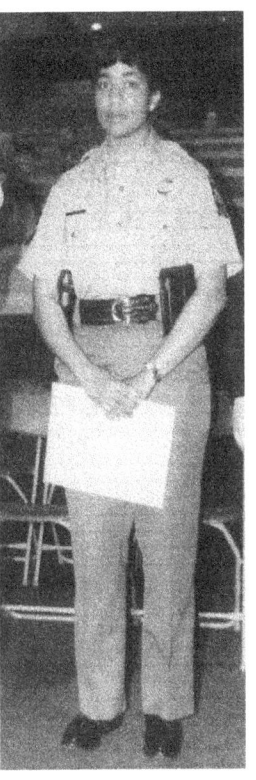

Sergeant Angela Palmer.
Courtesy of Palmer family.

"I was promoted to sergeant in January 2000 as supervisor in charge of the Civil Process/Judgment and Execution Unit, and Civilian Law Enforcement specialists under the special operations division. I was supervisor over the Fugitives and Extradition Unit and Civilian Law Enforcement specialists under the special operation division.

"I was also a supervisor over the warrant division and over general court security, and supervisor of two district squads with the uniform patrol division. My overall duties included administrative duties, supervising assigned staff, managing cases and calls for service, performing equipment maintenance and inspections and overseeing employees for professional development. I watched men who I supervised as a sergeant get promoted to lieutenant over me for no other reason than being white, so I decided on an early retirement from the sheriff's office." Many more officers like Palmer left. The list goes on.

I WAS THE LIEUTENANT in charge of the North Area District in 1989, when the homicide of an African American female cab driver, Geraldine Tisdale, occurred in the Union Heights area of North Charleston. Detective Tom Anderson and another detective were assigned to the case. Anderson used this opportunity to investigate me in hopes of finding evidence that I was corrupt and taking bribes instead of investigating the murder of Ms. Tisdale. The murder of Ms. Tisdale is a double tragedy because, as a result of Anderson's vindictiveness against me, her murder remains unsolved.

First, Anderson picked up an informant I used in Union Heights under the pretense of questioning him about his knowledge of Ms. Tisdale's murder. Anderson and a young white male detective took the informant to headquarters. However, Detective Anderson changed the subject and began questioning him about any knowledge the informant had of me taking bribes.

The informant's statement revealed that he said, "Anderson, man, you must be crazy. Lieutenant Frazier is tough but fair. If we violate the law, that person is arrested, and he does not take money." The informant went on to say in his statement, "Detective Tom Anderson don't like you and is trying to destroy your reputation."

I questioned the young, white detective who was with Anderson. He told me the information said was true and he wanted no part of it.

This was when I realized that Detective Tom Anderson had the blessing of a high command staff officer in the department, though no command staff officers would admit that an investigation of me was being conducted. The female major in charge of internal affairs also denied any knowledge of an investigation. Simply put, there were no official complaints or reasons for an investigation of me under department policy or procedure. I knew this investigation was due to my stance on racial discrimination of African Americans.

Charleston County Police / Sheriff's Office

SHERIFF ALTON J. CANNON

The year 1990 brought a substantial change to the Charleston County Police Department. The citizens of Charleston County voted to abolish the Charleston County Police Department, and as of January 1991, all law enforcement was placed under the jurisdiction of the Charleston County Sheriff's Office. There had been too many problems with corruption and politics in the Charleston County Police Department and Charleston County Council, and the governing body got tired of it. The vote passed by a narrow margin. As a result, Chief William J. Sidoran's position was abolished. Alton J. Cannon was sheriff when the change took effect in January 1991. All criminal law enforcement offenses prior to 1990 fell under the jurisdiction of the Charleston County Police Department. During that time, the sheriff's office oversaw the courts, county jail, prisoners, property tax and serving of civil papers.

MANY OF THE SAME command staff officers with racist views remained with the department. They continued trying to protect the status quo. It was obvious to me that Sergeant Tom Anderson and Major Edward Whitlock started rumors that I was taking money from drug dealers. Sergeant Anderson's informant was " S.G.2," one of the two men who I had arrested for burglary, rape and murder of a white female, Leolya Joy Key, in 1982. She lived in the Westchester subdivision of James Island. The informant pleaded guilty to misprisonment of a felony and was sentenced to the South Carolina Department of Corrections for ten years after he testified against his codefendant, Cody Conyers, who was sentenced to life. S.G.2 was sent to prison a second time after my investigation for a parole violation.

Tom Anderson convinced two high command staff officers in 1991 that he could solve Patrolman William Cribb's murder that had occurred on November 15, 1974, some sixteen years earlier. He leaned heavily on an informant, "B.C.1." I had previously charged B.C.1 with breaking and entering and grand larceny. Detective Sergeant George Gathers and I had interviewed him concerning his knowledge of the Cribb murder back in 1974. He knew nothing at the time and did not have any knowledge when he was sentenced to prison.

Later, Anderson apparently became acquainted with S.G.2 after his release from prison. He became Anderson's informant and convinced him that he knew who murdered Cribb. He supplied Anderson with the names of three suspects. However, those three suspects would have been thirteen to fifteen years old in November 1974. At the time of the murder, the local news media had written several stories describing the suspects as black males between the ages of nineteen and twenty-two; one was described as having pockmarks on his face. The three boys the informant named lived two blocks from my residence. If the sheriff's department had arrested those three boys, they would have been in for a rude awakening. Fortunately, Lieutenant Mickey Whatley, a SLED agent, informed high officials in the sheriff's office that Detective Anderson did not know what he was doing.

ON ANOTHER OCCASION, ANDERSON tried to set me up. Months before this, a James Island woman asked me to recommend her for employment with the Charleston County Police Department. I wouldn't do so because, although she was a former employee of the City of Charleston Police Department, she was a known drug user and an informant for the city police. Anderson and a black detective (who Chief Reuben Greenberg refused to promote) placed a recording device in her handbag, and she tried to get me to admit to some things I knew nothing about. When the investigation of me failed, the black detective was assisted in getting a job on the railroad to get away from the department. I understood why Chief Greenberg refused to promote this man. Anyone who calls himself a detective should know the difference between a statement, an allegation and evidence.

I was aware of Anderson's investigation and every move he made. This was despite the fact that there was no evidence that I did anything wrong while performing my duties as a police officer. I felt sorry for the black detective. He appeared to have a plantation mentality or the "Willie Lynch Syndrome." He was one of those black men who has to be patted on the back by a white man and told he did a good job before he can believe in himself. I hope by now he is aware of this. Later, he admitted to Captain Chevalier Harris and me that they were reporting directly to Sheriff Alton Cannon. After Tom Anderson's investigation of me failed, he also left the sheriff's office in shame and joined another department in South Carolina.

Three months before my decision to retire, I knew I had to make a choice before a tragedy occurred. My immediate supervisor, Captain James "Jim" Atchinson, radioed me and requested that I meet him at the Piggly Wiggly parking lot on Highway 7. Jim exited his cruiser and stood approximately ten feet away and waved for me to join him. He told me that he felt certain command staff officers were investigating me, and it had to be approved at the top, but they tried to hide it from him, and I knew the reason they would want me out.

I WOULD NOT KNOW until many years later the weight my career put on my family. There were many nights when I would come home after my 11:00 p.m. shift, put my key in the lock and realize that the door was unlocked. I had suspected that my daughter Geraldine, whose bedroom was closest to the front door, was peering out of her window until I drove up. She would see the light of my unmarked car, run to the door and unlock it. I realized my suspicion was correct because I caught her one night as she ran into her bedroom. Meanwhile, unbeknownst to us until a few years ago, my daughter Angela was peering out of her window as I drove up.

I also knew my wife, Mary, often worried and prayed for my safe return each night. But Mary was able to handle the stress of being the wife of a career police officer with such strength and in such a dignified and gracious manner that sometimes today I am still amazed by her.

Perhaps it was good that I did not fully realize the extent of their concern. The situation with my daughters and my wife might have affected earlier decisions regarding my career. But I was a tough cop. I believed I could handle myself. I was not going to let fear consume me, and I did my best to make sure my family was safe. I became know as the "Hunter Bear" and the "Enforcer" outside of my home. But I turned the switch off when I came home. Inside my house, I was and still am a big Teddy bear. I wanted my family to feel safe and loved so outside the house the Hunter Bear and the Enforcer status remained. But inside my house, I was the big Teddy bear that they can still wrap around their fingers.

ULTIMATELY, MY MEETING WITH Atchinson was the last straw. After that, I made the decision to retire. I had served approximately two years in the sheriff's office and had twenty-three years of unbleminshed service at the Charleston County Police Department. I also had six years of military service paid into the retirement system, which made me eligible for a thirty-one-year retirement. I decided to leave before a tragedy occurred. I had reached the point where any decision I made, with the exception of retiring, would not be in the best interest of my family. Thus, I retired in

Lieutenant Eugene Frazier with Dr. Charles Wallace at retirement ceremony. *Courtesy of author.*

1991, though I was just fifty-three years old. The county council chairman, Dr. Charles Wallace, congratulated me, and a resolution was placed in county council's record for my numerous accomplishments. It is an honor that very few employees have received.

The following are some of the murder cases that highlight my career.

Victim	Year	Defendant	Years Executed
Herman Simmons	1973	David Middleton	Life
Clarence Watson	1973	Frank Middleton	Life
Robert Munford	1973	David Middleton	Life
James Freeman	1973	Robert Frasier	Life

Victim	Year	Defendant	Years Executed
Ester K. Sanderlin	1975	Perry Deveau	Thirty years
John Ellerbee	1976	Kenneth Jones	Life
Rhonda Smith	1977	Leroy Drayton	1996 (Executed)
Michael Case	1977	Marvin Spell	Life
Calup Haynes	1977	Jesse C. Robinson	Life
Annette Young Lee	1978	Sammie L Butler	Life
Esdoran Friendly	1978	Sammie L. Butler	Life
Alvin Evans	1978	Sammie L. Butler	Life
Thomas Watkins	1978	Lawrence Rabon	Twenty-five years
Pamela L. Lane	1980	Horace Butler	Life
Brian K. Johnson	1980	Gary Davis	Thirty years to life
Lucia Aimar	1984	Earl Matthews	1997 (Executed)
Betty Gardner	1986	Frank Middleton	1997 (Executed)
Shirley M. Mack	1986	Frank Middleton	1997 (Executed)
Leola Joy Key	1982	Franklin Nelson	Life (now released)

I am proud of my work for the Charleston County Police Department and the sheriff's office. I always tried to stay prepared to deal with any situation. Toward that end, I earned the following certifications and diplomas: FBI In-Service Crime Scene Investigation; FBI Hostage Negotiation School located at the Citadel; FBI Advance Hostage Negotiation School located in Myrtle Beach, South Carolina; FBI Firearm Training; FBI Supervisory School; A.T.F. Treasury Training; National Auto Theft-White Collar Crime in Tallahassee, Florida; S.C. Criminal Justice Academy; Detective Class Criminal Justice Academy; Homicide Investigation; Forensic Homicide Crime Scene Investigation M.U.S.C. Hospital; Arson Investigation; Charleston County Management Essential; Managing Criminal Investigation; and the FBI Sex Offense Training. As

I have said, I was honored with the Police Officer of the Year award by the Exchange Club in 1972 and 1988 and Police Officer of the Month in February and March 1976. I also attended numerous classes at Trident Technical College during the '80s.

Soon after I retired from the county, I was hired by the U.S. Marshal Service at the federal district court in Charleston. I worked there for eight years. I would serve six of those years under Israel Brooks's administration. Our interactions were limited, as he worked in the main office located in Columbia, but just the idea of working for him was an honor because he was a man whom I held in high esteem.

My Time at the Federal Court

I was hired by the U.S. Marshal Service in 1992. I was a Court Security Officer (CSO) for the United States District Courthouse for the District of South Carolina, Charleston Division, located on Broad and Meeting Streets. I was also assigned to Columbia, Florence and Beaufort District Courthouses whenever additional staff was needed. My duties included security for the courthouse entrances, the courtrooms and the judges.

I enjoyed my eight-year employment with the Marshal Service. It allowed me the opportunity to get to know several of the federal judges assigned to the Charleston Courthouse. Judge Falcon B. Hawkins was one of the judges who I got to know personally. I highly respected Judge Hawkins because he was authentic and knew how to put people at ease. I had several conversations with Judge Hawkins in his chamber. During one of those conversations, I realized that he knew that his nephew, Paul Hawkins, and I had worked on many cases together in the police department. He commented on my relationship with Paul. Paul and I got along very well. I will never forget that Paul was the one who told me about Anderson's underhanded actions against me.

The judge also talked about his friend Senator Ernest Fritz Hollings. Senator Hollings recommended and nominated Judge Hawkins for the federal judgeship position. He was really proud of Fritz. He also knew of my relationship with Senator Hollings and his second wife Peatsy Liddy. My family worked for the Liddy family when I attended Burke High School and Fritz was the governor of South Carolina, before his senate election. In 1966, after Fritz was elected to the U.S. Senate, he and his wife, Peatsy, kept up with my career by mailing congratulations cards from Washington, D.C., on my various promotions and community awards.

Judge David C. Norton was another one of the federal court judges. I knew him prior to becoming a CSO. Before his district court appointment, he was a prosecutor with the Ninth Circuit Solicitor Office in state court. Judge Norton always impressed me as a straightforward type of man. He was quiet, logical and impartial and had great temperament and patience during deliberations. I found Judge Norton to be fair and impartial when dealing with defendants, regardless of race.

Judge Blatt was also one of the judges in whose courtroom I was assigned. I also found Judge Blatt to be a methodical, quiet, no-nonsense man. He was known for his appearance and attire. He was a very sharp and dapper dresser. I often noticed Judge Blatt in the courtroom paying close attention to the attorneys and clients. He was a stickler for details and would not hesitate to correct an attorney if needed. Judge Blatt's marshal preference was Fred Stroble. Judge Blatt and Fred had a special friendship, and he relied on Fred with secret and confidential information more than any other marshal.

Another district judge I held in high esteem was Judge Matthew Perry. Prior to being employed by the police department, I met Judge Perry in 1963, when he was an attorney representing the NAACP during the civil rights era in Charleston. He later earned the respect of Chief District Judge Robert Martin and many of the other jurists who he would join on the bench. Judge Perry was a master in the courtroom. He possessed an eloquent baritone voice and had a wealth of knowledge about the law. When I sat in his courtroom listening to him, I was spellbound. He had me mesmerized, and I observed that the audience seemed mesmerized as well.

3
HONORS

My time with the Charleston County Police Department and then the Charleston County Sheriff's Office introduced me to a number of outstanding individuals—black and white, male and female, old and young, who took great pride in their work and accomplished much. I have named several of them already, but I want to be sure that the following are also highlighted. I was especially proud of my lawsuit that brought about the hiring of black females, and as a result, I became a mentor to many of them. I believe that this mentoring aspect of my life has been rewarding.

Jesse Washington was hired by the Charleston City Police Department in November 1980. The city police department and the patrol area were broken into several teams. During an interview I conducted with Jessie, he said, "Frazier, I worked in every team in the department over the years. A memorable day was December 7, 1997, when I received a call to investigate a suspicious person on the Cooper River Bridge, who was possibly trying to commit suicide. I observed a white male on the bridge threatening to jump off. I talked him out of jumping and got him the help he needed.

"I resigned from the city police department in February 1997 and went to work for McDougall Correctional Institution. I worked as a transport officer until I retired with twenty years of law enforcement service in the year 2000. Lieutenant, I have to say that I enjoyed my law enforcement career—after all, it was you who encouraged me to become a police officer."

INTEGRATING THE CHARLESTON POLICE FORCE

PFC Jesse Washington with Chief Reuben Greenberg. *Courtesy of family.*

I said, "Jesse, I am guilty to that charge."

He continued, "Frazier, Reuben Greenberg and I did not always see eye to eye before I left the department, but I did respect him, and he had those same words for me regardless of our differences, he respected me."

Walter Mitchell grew up on James Island. Following his graduation from South Carolina State College, he began his career playing professional football for the Pittsburgh Steelers and then in the World Football League.

He began a second career when he returned home to Charleston. He was hired by the Charleston County Sheriff's Office in 1974 and served there until 1976. In 1976, he was appointed as agent with the South Carolina State Law Enforcement Division, making him the third African American from Charleston County to do so. Mitchell was dispatched to several police departments in South Carolina during his career. He assisted local police during many high-profile investigations, including the 1984 murder investigation of Earl Matthews in Charleston County, which I discussed earlier.

Walter Mitchell retired from SLED in 1992 with the rank of lieutenant. He operated Mitchell Investigation Service in the Goose Creek and

Honors

Above: SLED agent Walter Mitchell standing by auto. *Courtesy of Mitchell family.*

Left: *Left to right*: Eugene Frazier, U.S. marshal Fred Stroble and Walter Mitchell at Fred's retirement. *Courtesy of U.S. deputy marshal Fred Stroble.*

metropolitan Charleston County areas after his retirement. Recently, Walter Mitchell and I were honored among one hundred honorees with the Martin Luther King Dream Keepers Award. It was an honor and a privilege for both of us to be singled out in this manner.

Betty Ann Rowlin was hired in 1972 by Chief John Conroy of the City of Charleston Police Department. I knew her during her career working with the city police department.

Betty began our interview by saying, "Frazier, when I was first hired, I was placed in charge of the meter maids, handling parking violations. I was certified as a police officer after completing my training, and later, I was appointed supervisor in charge of the police cadet program in the city police department. I worked with the program for almost twenty years as a supervisor. I oversaw many of those cadets who would later become veteran police officers. I even helped to train one of your protégés, Victor Hill. I decided to retire after serving almost twenty years with the city police department and began my second career in the private sector."

Tusha R. Lafayette is another young African American female from James Island who I encouraged to consider a career in law enforcement. In our interview, she said, "Frazier, I began my career with the North Charleston City Police Department in 1998, as a patrol officer. I was assigned as a school resource officer, which afforded me the opportunity to make a lasting impact on the lives of students attending high school in the city of North Charleston from 1999 to 2006. I was appointed to manage the police department's youth court program due to my strong ability to relate to students.

"This voluntary division program allowed first-time offenders of nonviolent crimes an opportunity to be tried by their true peers. I assumed the responsibility of recruiting, training and supervising service-learning projects as a youth court coordinator. I traveled to various states to participate in conferences to collaborate and brainstorm with other agencies on ways to enhance the program.

I was later transferred to the investigation division to conduct criminal investigations on an array of cases, such as sexual assault, murder, larceny, malicious injury to property and assault and battery. My strong background dealing with juveniles and investigations prompted me to apply for an investigator position with the prosecutor's office. I became a special investigator for the family court division in 2006. I worked closely

Honors

PFC Tusha R. Lafayette.
Courtesy of Tusha R. Lafayette.

with four juvenile prosecutors who handled cases from all law enforcement agencies throughout the county."

As of publication, Tusha is still employed with the Charleston County Family Court Solicitor's Office.

Priscilla Bell Sarpy was hired by Chief John Conroy to the Charleston City Police Department in 1977. Priscilla and I had many discussions while we were working as court security officers with the U.S. Marshal Service.

She said, "Eugene, I worked for the city police department until 1989. Because I had enough of how we were treated as African Americans, especially as a female officer, I resigned. I was hired by the Medical University of South Carolina as a state constable and was employed with them for eight years. I resigned from that position and accepted a position as CSO with the

U.S. Marshal Court Security Service at Broad and Meeting in Charleston, where I worked with you and many others. I retired after serving twenty-four years in law enforcement."

Janet O. Bolds began her career in law enforcement in 1990 with the Charleston County Police Department. She told me, "I worked as an identification technician for three years. Later, I joined the Mount Pleasant Police Department. I held several positions while employed there, including patrol officer, crime scene technician, evidence custodian and police corporal. I became the first black female corporal and field training officer."

She added, "I immediately encountered racism from the citizens of the town of Mount Pleasant. The comments included, 'Oh, we did not know that they hired you people to work in the town' or being called a 'nigger' when making an arrest. Race was a factor in promotions and duty. Captain Frank Riccio would ask me not to cross my arms over my chest because people were intimidated by me. I received bogus complaints during my career," she continued.

"While working as a corporal, I was taking the test for sergeant, and a black officer said to me, 'You would go far at Mount Pleasant Police Department if you learned to play the game.'

"I knew exactly where he was going and told him that I was not going to play games for nobody. I became pregnant, and it was suggested to me since I was not married, I should put a wedding ring on my finger to make people believe that I was married. I left the Mount Pleasant Police department in 1995, after I gave birth to my son because of a personal matter."

I knew **Debbie Glover** since she was a young child. Her mother, father, sister and brothers lived less than a city block from where I grew up. Debbie and my daughter Geraldine were childhood friends. Debbie graduated from James Island High School in 1978. She attended St. Augustine University and graduated in 1982.

Debbie came to me in 1983 and told me she was considering joining the North Charleston Police Department. She would become one of several African American females from James Island who I encouraged to get involved in law enforcement. I was really proud of her. Debbie had a calm, quiet demeanor, and I believed that she would make a good police officer.

Years later, Debbie called and asked me to come to her home on Riverland Drive. She informed me that she had cancer. I tried to comfort

Honors

Left: PFC Deborah Glover. *Courtesy of Georgette Glover.*

Right: PFC Deborah Glover and Marie Henderson and husband. *Courtesy of Georgetta Glover.*

her because I had gone through seven months of chemo for colon cancer. However, she told me that her case was terminal. I was crushed. She died several months later.

My daughter Geraldine was living in Norfolk, Virginia, and was unable to attend the funeral. She sent a letter to me titled "A Tribute to Debbie" and asked me to read it at the funeral. I was so hurt that I was unable to read it, but Kim Seymour, a cousin and friend of the family, read the tribute at the funeral for me.

Sheila Santos was a childhood friend of my daughter Angela. She said her decision to become a police officer was because of me. In a message to my daughter Geraldine, Sheila said, "Mr. Frazier is a huge part of my love of the law."

She added,

INTEGRATING THE CHARLESTON POLICE FORCE

As a child aged 11, I would watch him talk about his work with such passion and with every word, I knew I was going to walk in his footsteps. He knew his job, and he did it with such professionalism. I wanted to be just like him. He was like a second dad to me. He's the best, and I owe it all to him. I started at the very bottom as a Safety Service Officer with the City of Charleston Police Department. I began working in the Correctional field throughout the State of South Carolina and Virginia. I also clerked for a bond court judge. However, my travels with the military put my career on hold at times. Today, I am employed with the Charleston County Sheriff's Department where I am assigned to the Charleston County Courthouse as a Limited Duty Deputy. Mr. Frazier touched my life in such a great way. My passion for law is all due to him. I am forever grateful; because of him, I was able to fulfill my dream of working in Law Enforcement. I made my mom and dad proud each time I was recognized for my work. I salute Mr. Frazier. I love him.

I just found out a few months ago about Sheila's appreciation for me. As a police officer, we can inspire young people to achieve their goals. Police officers were often admired and revered when Sheila was a child. Those feelings of admiration and appreciation are lacking today. But as police officers, we should not forget that we are role models to so many. We must choose to carry our badge with as much honor and dignity as possible.

Detective Corporal Cheryl Gadsden Byrd. *Courtesy of Louis M. Byrd.*

John H. Ball from James Town, New York, was chief of the Charleston County Police Department in 1975. I was a detective corporal at the time. My first assignment from Chief Ball was to find and interview qualified African American male and female candidates and submit their names for employment. There were no black female officers on the force at the time. The first two females I interviewed and recommended for the job were **Cheryl Gadsden Byrd** and Gwendolyn Frazier (no relationship to me). They were both hired after background investigations and after passing background tests and written and physical exams. Cheryl worked in the uniform patrol division, and over the years, she was promoted to corporal. She had an easygoing personality that generated friendships and camaraderie in any group. Officer Byrd is now deceased due to health-related complications.

Marilyn Wallace was hired as a City of Charleston police officer by Chief John Conroy in 1973. Wallace became the second African American female in the history of the department. Marilyn served several years with the city police department before she resigned. She was then hired by the Charleston County Police Department and served several years before leaving for a civilian position.

ATHOUGH THE 1950s THROUGH the 1990s were trying and difficult times for African American police officers, I must say that there were several white officers who treated me with respect during those early years. I would be remiss if I did not mention some of them. I know some were not well liked by members of the department because of their relationship with me. These men and women are as follows:

Detective James "Jimmy" Robinson was from James Island. He was one of those white men who was rare to find in law enforcement during those turbuluent years between the 1960s and the 1970s. The racial situation between blacks and whites was not good during those years. But Jimmy believed in equal treatment regardless of race.

During those years, there were only three African American patrolmen on the force to cover the three shifts from 7:00 a.m. to 3:00 p.m., 3:00 p.m. to 11:00 p.m. and 11:00 p.m. to 7:00 a.m. Sometimes I did not have a partner, but Jimmy would volunteer to partner with me in a two-man team, especially during the midnight shift. He was asked by white officers why he wanted to ride with a nigger.

Jimmy knew I was a veteran of the U.S. Army, had served for six years and was honorably discharged as a sergeant. When Jimmy discovered his salary was higher than mine, although we were in the same pay grade, he told me. I complained to the assistant chief, but the only thing he wanted to know was where I got the information concerning pay. Jimmy did not back down. He told the supervisor that he told me.

I socialized with Jimmy many times during those years, even at his residence. Jimmy spent several years with the Charleston County Police Department. After resigning from the department, he was hired by SLED

Integrating the Charleston Police Force

Right: Officer James Robinson. *Courtesy of James Robinson.*

Below: Detective James Robinson and Detective Eugene Frazier. *Courtesy of James Robinson.*

Honors

as a state alcoholic beverage control agent. He also worked in conjuction with Alcohol Tobacco Firearms (ATF) for several years. Jim ended his law enforcement career and opened his own successful bail bonding company. Robinson Bail Bonding Company is family owned and operated. The company is still in operation, has a good reputation and is located in North Charleston across from the Sheriff Al Cannon Detention Center. Jimmy and I remain friends to this day.

Chief Ronald "Roddy" Perry.
Courtesy of Perry family.

Lieutenant Michael Whatley, second in command of the detective division, was determined that I receive credit for my dedicated detective work. I worked with him beginning in the early 1960s and associated with him throughout his career, until his death. Michael Whatley, who everyone in the department affectionately called "Mickey," was a white man born and raised in the South during the segregation era when African Americans were treated as second-class citizens. It was rare to find white policemen with the ethical standards that Mickey possessed when dealing with African Americans, treating them the same as he did whites. Mickey was truly a man of integrity beyond reproach. He later became chief of the North Charleston Police Department and a SLED agent.

Detective Ronald "Roddy" Perry, who was my partner for eight years, worked homicides and robberies. He later became chief of the Mount Pleasant Police Department.

Captain James Atchinson, along with SLED agent Lieutenant Michael Whatley, alerted me of the investigation being conducted against me.

Detective Lieutenant Paul Hawkins told me when he learned from Tom Anderson, who was trying to set me up, that his informant was S.G.2. Hawkins said he told Anderson that the informant was a manipulator, a lying SOB and could not be trusted.

Integrating the Charleston Police Force

Lieutenant Maxey Baxter, **Sergeant Curt Parsley**, **Sergeant James "Duke" Harley**, **Lieutenant Andy York**, **Corporal William Tolson**, and **Lieutenant Bobby Minter** were all men I highly respected.

I also include **Captain Joyce Kephart Todd** in this group. She once worked in my squad and was promoted to captain before she retired. She was a dedicated, professional police officer, true to the cause, and someone a supervisor could rely on. I went against many of my white command staff officers when I supported her before the Sergeant Promotonial Board. Many of the officers were against her being promoted. I still maintain a cordial relationship with her because of my respect for her and vice versa.

Another officer was **Barry Goldstein**, who, when I worked with him, was a detective with the Charleston City Police Department. As of this writing he is a detective with the sheriff's office.

WITH THE EXCEPTION OF those men and women listed above, I lost respect for the entire command staff officers with the ranks of captain, major and deputy chief who served under William J. Sidoran and Sheriff Al Cannon during my tour. This also includes the lone African American, the late deputy chief who stood by and allowed these African American men and women to be discriminated against and said and did nothing to assist me or help them.

Times are slowly changing, but change was really evident in North Charleston when **Reginald L. Burgess** was elevated to the position of chief of police for the North Charleston Police Department.

Reggie represents a new era in Charleston. He is the first black chief of police for the North Charleston Police Department and only the second black police chief since Chief Rueben Greenberg. In January 2018, Reginald Burgess inherited a department that was charged with discrimination tactics against blacks and increasing gun violence. He inherited the office less than three years after the Walter Scott murder. It was a turbulent time, but I believe Reggie is the best man for the job. He grew up in the Liberty Hill section of North Charleston,

North Charleston police chief Reginald L. Burgess. *Courtesy of Geraldine F. Minter.*

and he knows the city. He will make a positive difference in his community. He has shown that he cares, and I have found that is one key ingredient for success in a police department. The people must know that their police department cares about them. The residents in North Charleston know that Reggie cares. He is one of them.

I ALSO WANT TO give my thanks and appreciation to some of the attorneys for their support from the early years of my law enforcement career to the present. I value the professional and social advice they gave me throughout the years. Their advice helped me survive some of the most difficult years of my career. I lived to retire with thirty-four years in law enforcement. I will never forget any of them.

Gedney Main Howe Jr. was known as a "Lawyer's Lawyer." I spent many hours in his office on King Street near Broad Street during the 1960s through the 1970s, as we discussed the social issues of our country and the world. I became mesmerized while listening to him in his law library. He was the most fascinating, articulate and brilliant lawyer I had ever had conversations with. Gedney explained to me why men such as Mohandas Gandhi and Dr. Martin Luther King Jr. taught their philosophies and tried to bring change to the world. He explained that it was because of the unjust treatment of the poor that existed in every country and nation. He added that Dr. King's journey to Mecca in the Holy Land to study Gandhi's nonviolent philosophies helped him tremendously in the civil rights movement in this country.

Gedney explained that history revealed that it takes a variety of men with different ideologies to make a democratic society work. He added that, as far as individual rights were concerned, the right to vote, freedom of speech and other unalienable rights observed in this country are surpassed by none. He added that every country has underprivileged individuals who the wealthy in society sometimes forget.

Gedney said, "Men in power such as the late FBI director J. Edger Hover began their careers crusading against causes that were evil and detrimental to society and made tremendous contributions. But," he added, "Hoover was allowed too much power, and no one man should ever again possess and control the amount of power that Hoover held because of the potential for abuse."

Integrating the Charleston Police Force

Attorney Gedney Main Howe III.
Courtesy of Gedney Howe.

Gedney M. Howe III, as I always say, is a chip off the old block. He is just like his father. On numerous occasions, I sought and received sound legal advice during those problematic years in the 1970s through 1991. Gedney Howe was instrumental in handling the controversy surrounding the termination of Major Michael Boggs and the appointment of Thomas Dawson as assistant chief of police by Chief William Sidoran in 1988. Thanks to his knowledge and expertise dealing with county government, he saw that Michael Boggs received a position equivalent to a major in county government. This resulted in no retaliation against any police officers. Most of the police officers during that time appreciated Gedney's involvement in bringing this matter to a satisfactory conclusion.

Years later, it was be Gedney who helped me when I found myself the target of an unfounded investigation. Anyone who becomes an activist, willingly or unwillingly, must be prepared to be a target. I knew it would happen. I told Gedney about finding out that I might be target. He immediately contacted one of his friends to look out for me. Gedney was a friend in those dark days.

Charleston was and still is a place where the color of your skin can make all the difference. A black person with a 4.0 GPA, multiple degrees and possessing a key position in the community would not have been able to help me because skin color would be a hinderance. Gedney could get the job done, though. He knew it and so did I. I did not have to comment on his race affording him this opportunity. There was no need to.

Recently, my daughter had a conversation with one of her friends who was elected to an office in Charleston. Her friend, who is white, told her about meeting with an activist who needed assistance with bringing help, such as cleanup, to a playground. She told my daughter, "I hope the day comes when black people do not have to come to a white person to get things done in Charleston. They can get it done themselves." They both know that today this is not the reality, but it is my belief that one day it will be.

One day, I visited Gedney, who had just become the owner of the building next door to his office. He took me inside the building, and I have never forgotten the feeling and emotions that I felt as we walked inside. The building was 8 Chalmers Street and is known as the Old Slave Mart.

The significance of this building lies in its history,

> *Throughout the first half of the 19th century, slaves brought into Charleston were sold at public auctions held on the north side of the Exchange and Provost building. After the city prohibited public slave auctions in 1856, enclosed slave markets sprang up along Chalmers, State, and Queen Streets. One such market was Ryan's Mart, established by City Councilman and broker Thomas Ryan and his business partner James Marsh. Ryan's Mart originally consisted of a closed lot with three structures—a four-story barracoon or slave jail, a kitchen, and a morgue or "dead house." In 1859, an auction master named Z.B. Oakes purchased Ryan's Mart and built what is now the Old Slave Mart building for use as an auction gallery. The building's auction table was 3 feet (0.91 m) high and 10 feet (3.0 m) long and stood just inside the arched doorway. In addition to slaves, the market sold real estate and stock. Slave auctions at Ryan's Mart were advertised in broadsheets throughout the 1850s, some appearing as far away as Galveston, Texas.*

The floor was still dirt at that time, and as I walked in and stood on that floor, the emotion that it evoked in me was like nothing I had ever felt before. I know that, somehow, I was feeling the misery, pain and fear of my ancestors. It is a feeling that I will never forget.

Arnold Goodstein is an attorney and a former member of county council who challenged the county police policy and Captain Richard F. Grassie concerning the frame-up of me during the early 1970s. The grand jury refused to indict me, and Councilman Goodstein saw that I returned to duty.

Andrew Savage III is a former prosecutor with the fifth circuit and the ninth circuit solicitor's offices. He is now one of the state's greatest defense lawyers. He is not afraid to dig up the truth, no matter where it leads. After I retired, I did private investigative work for the Savage Law Firm.

One of the investigations led to Andy's creation of "The A-Team." The A-Team consisted of James Randolph, Robert Minter, Bill Capps and me. We were instrumental in solving the murder of Kate Waring. The case aired on *Dateline*, in a segment titled, "Stranger on a Train."

Integrating the Charleston Police Force

The A Team: Bill Capp, Eugene Frazier Sr., James Randolph and Robert Minter. *Courtesy of Andrew J Savage.*

During one of our conversations, Andy confirmed the statement made by then-Captain Richard F. Grassie in 1976, when he referred to Detective Sergeant George Gathers and me as "niggers." It gave me great satisfaction knowing that despite having to be in the company of men who held similar views as Grassie, Andy did not become tainted. He is still a man with integrity and credibility, and I consider him a special friend.

We recently met to say goodbye to our friend Fred Stroble at Fred's homegoing service. Andy gave his remarks during the funeral service, and I gave my remarks at Fred's wake. Andy provided a good look into the heart of Fred. Fred was a man who was devoted to his faith, his job, his family and his friends. Andy and Fred know what true friendship is all about.

For years now, sometime during the month of November, I will get gifts of some of the best fruits I have ever tasted from Andy. My family and I all gather around to get our pick of this special treat. There are many others who also receive this delectable treat from Andy. He does not forget his friends. He has helped so many people.

More than thirty-five years ago, my daughter asked him for a reference letter. He did not hesitate for a second. When I told Andy about this writing project, he offered to help, and he did. John Lennon once said, "Being honest may not get you a lot of friends, but it'll always get you the right ones." My life in law enforcement did not get me a lot of friends and often brought me enemies, but Andy was one of the right ones. I am thankful for that.

Honors

IN THE 1960s THROUGH the 1970s, few white lawyers defended any black clients. Poor blacks who were charged with crimes and were unable to afford an attorney were declared indigent and appointed representation by the court from the Charleston County Public Defender's Office. I must take my hat off to the first groups of white public defender lawyers who were appointed in Charleston County to defend the indigent. I consider them pioneers in more ways than one. Among these lawyers were **Michael P. O'Connell**, **G. Dan Bowling**, **Dale Cobb** and **William Runyon**. They were trailblazers who gave 100 percent. They defended their clients with the intensity of lawyers who had been paid thousands of dollars.

They were, in my opinion, instrumental in pushing police officers to become professionals. Police officers soon realized that these public defenders meant business. They scrutinized and challenged evidence and confessions in a vigorous manner never before seen by police in Charleston County. This caused many police officers to think twice before crossing that thin line between right and wrong.

Michael P. O'Connell is a U.S. Army veteran of the Vietnam War. Before moving to Charleston in 1977, Michael spent many years in the Richland County Public Defender Office. In 1977, Michael moved to Charleston and began representing indigent clients in the Charleston County Public Defender's office. During his eight years in the public defender's office, he handled many of the robbery and murder cases in which I was the investigating detective.

In April 1991, Federal Public Defender Parks Small opened the federal public defender's office in Charleston. He hired Michael O'Connell to lead that office. One of Michael's first decisions was to interview and ultimately choose a legal assistant to work with him. His choice was my daughter Geraldine, who considers working with Michael as one of the greatest working experiences she has ever had. Michael demonstrated respect, compassion and understanding to all of the clients who came into that office during her employment. She witnessed Michael always giving 100 percent, and he

Attorney Michael P. O'Connell.
Courtesy of Michael O'Connell.

propelled her to do the same. During their first eight months—with only the two of them, no investigator, no other staff—Michael won a trial against the United States attorney's office. The trial involved a young man from the city of Charleston who was charged with possession of a firearm by a convicted felon. The sentence could be as much as five years. However, it was not a long deliberation. Michael was able to show the jury, as I mentioned before, that many people are wrongly arrested because of unscrupulous police officers. Because of the dedication of defense attorneys like Michael, a young man was not wrongly convicted.

My daughter recalled that after the jury announced the verdict and people were leaving the courtroom, Michael turned to the client and told him to be careful. He had just won a case against the city police department, and he should watch himself. The case might be over, but Michael's concern was not. I also witnessed Michael's display of concern for a client during a state court trial. The judge noticed and told Michael he had done all he could for the client, and he should not feel bad about his defense or performance. During Michael's combined service as a state and federal public defender, Michael worked on at least three death penalty appeal cases before he left for private practice. I was the investigator in at least two of those cases. Michael is, in my opinion, among the top defense lawyers in Charleston and truly a man with integrity and credibility. My family and I also consider Michael and his wife, Ann Stirling, friends.

During a time of personal struggle, it was Michael who we turned to. My daughter puts it this way, "Galatians 6:2 says, 'Carry each other's burdens, and in this way, you will fulfill the law of Christ.'" She saw Michael demonstrate this with his clients time and time again, and later, he would do the same for her. She still remembers one of their first clients praising them before being sentenced by Judge Sol Blatt Jr. The client praised both of them for helping to carry her burden during this period of her life—the first time she had ever been involved in the criminal justice system. The client received probation. My daughter said she sat with the defendant's mother, and they both wept. It seemed that easing the burden of their clients had become a part of Michael's role as an assistant federal public defender and, ultimately, my daughter's role as his legal assistant.

As I described earlier, **George A. Payton** was an up-and-coming African American attorney and a friend of mine. He was smart and looking to achieve greatness. He was not afraid to call white men on issues when they were wrong during those turbulent times of the late 1960s. But his life was cut short. He was murdered at a young age. It is one of those unsolved cases that haunts me for a number of circumstances, including the inability of investigators to follow proper police procedure, the refusal of help from other law enforcement officers who had the ability and proven success in this type of investigation and the racial prejudice and the political climate of the 1970s. Payton had all the tools to achieve greatness despite living in the segregated South.

Professor Damon L. Fordham's 2017 article gives a detailed look at a man who should be held in his rightful place as a civil rights icon in Charleston:

> *Over forty years before President Barack Obama's Affordable Health Care Act, Atty. Payton made this proposal in his campaign literature. "I believe that every man, woman, and child deserves the best quality of medical care possible. I do not believe that money should be a prerequisite for medical services. Therefore, I favor extending social security legislation to the extent that all medical expenditures of all citizens should be covered."*
>
> *He lost that election, but he ran for the state senate in 1974. He told a Georgetown audience that year, "I am interested in people issues that affect the lives of all. Old and young, black and white, rich and poor. We need people of good will together to form a coalition of conscience, a vanguard with the spirit de corps to stand up for candidates that will protect the rights of the people. With the building of a coalition of mutual respect and cooperation among the people…we can change the issues from special interests to the needs of the people."*
>
> *In spite of his losing that election also, he was a beloved figure among black Charlestonians. He was one of the few local leaders with education and articulation that would speak for those who could not speak for themselves and used his skills to improve the conditions of others. Another issue that he passionately fought for was the fight for poor people to save their land from wealthy realtors. It is widely believed that this was what led to the horrible events of March 18, 1975. During a telephone conversation with fellow attorney Joab Dowling, a black man entered his office on Spring Street and shot him to death. The murder was never solved, and his daughter Angel recently fought to have the case reopened. However, the Charleston Chronicle of March 29, 1975, showed what Payton's community felt about him. The paper reported that 10,000 local mourners attended his funeral at Morris Street Baptist Church.*

Integrating the Charleston Police Force

Judge Richard E. Fields.
Courtesy of Geraldine F. Minter.

I met **Judge Richard Fields** in 1966, in the Spring Street law office that he and Attorney George A. Payton shared. In 1969, I was a uniform patrolman with the Charleston County Police Department. I testified in many cases before him when he served as a municipal court judge in Charleston. In 1980, he was elected judge in the ninth circuit, and I also testified in many cases while he was the presiding judge. I have always found Judge Fields to be fair, impartial and easy to talk with. My last case in front of him was in 1981. At that time, defendant James Arnold was charged with armed robbery, assault with intent to kill and shooting into my unmarked cruiser. This case was investigated by Detective Barry Goldstein while he was with city police department.

CONCLUSION

My twenty-five-year career as a police officer has often been challenging, heartbreaking and chilling. It has been one heck of a roller coaster. But during that ride, there were moments of kindness, hope and love. One of those challenging days in 1969 really set the course for who I would become as a police officer. I was dispatched to assist two white officers who were enforcing an eviction at the EME Apartments on James Island. The manager of the complex was there along with the woman, who was crying. She was about to get evicted, and she had nowhere to go. Her two daughters were sitting with their belongings on the curb. I knew I had a choice to make. I could have done my job and enforced the eviction with the two white officers or I could try to be her hero. I chose the latter. After talking with her, I went to the manager and asked if there was any way he could allow the woman and her children to stay. They worked out a solution, and she was allowed to stay. That day I thought I was her hero. But, as noted in the *Chronicle* later that week, the woman did not refer to me as her hero. She referred to me as her angel.

We make a choice in every situation as police officers. Sometimes we have no choice but to do exactly what we are told, in accordance with the law. But there are so many opportunities when we are able to do our jobs and still become someone's hero or angel. No matter how bad my days were in law enforcement, the days that I became someone's hero will always shine bright for me. It is my hope that when you read this book, you will realize that my intentions are not to hurt anyone. I am simply speaking my truth. My career began during turbulent times in our history—the Jim Crow era and segregation. People were more authentic then—for good and for bad. They did not have to hide their beliefs and values like they do now. This authentic behavior is what made it possible for me to know my enemies. Today it is the opposite, and that makes life even tougher for police officers who are discriminated against.

Throughout my career, I only wanted black officers to be given an equal opportunity, because I knew if they were given the chance they would excel. I wanted us to be judged not by our race but by our character and performance. I hope this book will encourage all men and women in the criminal justice system to evaluate whether they are in the right career. Everyone makes mistakes, but the biggest mistake is to stay in a profession that is supposed to be justice for all when you don't believe in justice for all.

I am grateful for the love and support of my wonderful wife, Francis "Mary"; our children; our grandchildren; my parents, Sandy and Viola Frazier (both deceased); my wonderful sisters; and other family members and friends. It was this love and support, along with my faith in God, that helped me through some of those dark days.

Our world has no place for injustice and racism. I pray that we will see more officers choose careers in law enforcement because they want to make positive differences. The world can use more officers who choose to be angels when the opportunity presents itself and who refuse to succumb to the disease called racism. I have made my mark against racism and injustice, and sometimes it has cost my family and me. But I know that I would do it again.

For those of you who are in the criminal justice system, it is your chance to make a mark. I hope you will strike a blow against injustice and racism. The day will come when you will think over your life and answer whether you were part of the problem or part of the solution. I hope you can resoundingly say, "Yes, I was a part of the solution. I made a difference."

BIBLIOGRAPHY

Blakeney, Barney. "Asst. Chief Reggie Burgess Becomes North Charleston's Ninth Police Chief." *Charleston Chronicle,* January 10, 2018. https://www.charlestonchronicle.net.

Fordham, Damon L. "The Wisdom of Atty. George Payton." *Charleston Chronicle*, February 24, 2017.

Francis, C. "Officer Is Known as "Enforcer." *Evening Post*, February 1990.

Frazier, Eugene, Sr. *From Segregation to Integration: The Making of a Black Policeman*. Charleston, SC: The History Press, 2001.

Gardner, K. "Detective Unhurt with Armed Suspect." *Evening Post*, 1981.

Goodreads. "John Lennon Quotes." Retrieved September 14, 2019. https://www.goodreads.com.

"Old Slave Mart." Last modified September 1, 2019. https://en.wikipedia.org.

ABOUT THE AUTHOR

Eugene Frazier Sr. is married to the former Francis E. Prioleau. They have three children, six grandchildren and two great-grandchildren.

Mr. Frazier served six years in the United States Army and was honorably discharged as a Sergeant, E-6. Later, Mr. Frazier was employed as a police officer with the Charleston County Police Department. This employment spanned more than twenty-five years until his retirement as a police lieutenant with the Charleston County Sheriff's Office.

After his retirement, Mr. Frazier was employed for eight years with the United States Marshal Service as a court security officer (CSO).

Mr. Frazier is a member of Saint James Presbyterian Church and has served as a Sunday school teacher, chairman of the Men's Council and a former member of the trustee board. Presently, he is an active member of the organization designed to preserve and protect African American cemeteries on James Island. He is also a member of the Friends of McLeod, whose members are dedicated to preserving and protecting McLeod Plantation. Because of his dedication, a picture of Eugene Frazier Sr. is one of only four images selected to grace a room in the home at McLeod Plantation.

About the Author

He is a Thirty-Second Degree Mason and the past worshipful master of the Sons of Elijah Masonic Lodge no. 457. Mr. Frazier served for five years on the Charleston County Constituent School Board no. 3. As a board member, Mr. Frazier was a staunch supporter of quality education. He maintains an active involvement with the schools for presentation and volunteer work and remains dedicated to ensuring that all students get fair and equal treatment and education. James Island Elementary School is a testimony to the belief that Mr. Frazier is a hero for all ages, as he was proclaimed its Hero of the Month during one of its history programs.

Mr. Frazier is an active writer, historian, storyteller and community activist in his spare time. His books include *From Segregation to Integration: The Making of a Black Policeman*, *James Island: Stories from Slave Descendants* and *James Island Stories of Slave Descendants and Plantation Owners: The Bloodline*. On August 19, 2010, Eugene Frazier was inducted into the Avery Research Center as a donor in residence where his books, articles and some of his papers and research will be on display for all to enjoy.

In December 2011, Mr. Frazier was chosen as a merit winner by Payne United Methodist Church in its first annual award celebration for his contribution to the field of law enforcement, though Mr. Frazier is not even a member of the church. He was elected as the recipient of the Award of Merit by the Confederation of South Carolina Local Historical Societies in 2011. Mr. Frazier was also among a select group chosen in April 2011 to contribute an article to the *Charleston Magazine* for its discussion on the sesquicentennial celebration of the Civil War.

Further, James Island mayor Bill Woosley proclaimed May 7 as Eugene Frazier Sr. Day, due to his numerous accomplishments and dedication to his city. Mayor John Tecklenberg of the city of Charleston named Mr. Frazier the 2016 recipient of the Harold Koon Award, a city of Charleston award that is given annually by the mayor to a member of the community who demonstrated ongoing exemplary volunteer service to the community in the same tradition as Koon. In January 2018, Mr. Frazier was honored as the Lowcountry Hero of the Month by WTAT-TV Fox 24. The next month, Mr. Frazier was one of the honorees for the Dr. Martin Luther King's Dream Keeper Award. Mr. Frazier is available for educational and cultural events as a presenter and storyteller.

www.ingramcontent.com/pod-product-compliance
Lightning Source LLC
Chambersburg PA
CBHW042141160426
43201CB00021B/2363